The
Highest
Goal

The Highest Goal

**The Secret
That Sustains
You in Every
Moment**

Michael Ray

BK

BERRETT-KOEHLER PUBLISHERS, INC.
San Francisco

Berrett-Koehler Publishers, Inc.
235 Montgomery Street, Suite 650
San Francisco, CA 94104-2916
Tel: (415) 288-0260   Fax: (415) 362-2512   www.bkconnection.com

Ordering Information
Quantity sales. Special discounts are available on quantity purchases by corporations, associations, and others. For details, contact the "Special Sales Department" at the Berrett-Koehler address above.
Individual sales. Berrett-Koehler publications are available through most bookstores. They can also be ordered directly from Berrett-Koehler: Tel: (800) 929-2929; Fax: (802) 864-7626; www.bkconnection.com
Orders for college textbook/course adoption use. Please contact Berrett-Koehler: Tel: (800) 929-2929; Fax: (802) 864-7626.
Orders by U.S. trade bookstores and wholesalers. Please contact Publishers Group West, 1700 Fourth Street, Berkeley, CA 94710. Tel: (510) 528-1444; Fax (510) 528-3444.

Berrett-Koehler and the BK logo are registered trademarks of Berrett-Koehler Publishers, Inc.

Printed in the United States of America
Berrett-Koehler books are printed on long-lasting acid-free paper. When it is available, we choose paper that has been manufactured by environmentally responsible processes. These may include using trees grown in sustainable forests, incorporating recycled paper, minimizing chlorine in bleaching, or recycling the energy produced at the paper mill.

Library of Congress Cataloging-in-Publication Data
Ray, Michael L.
    The highest goal : the secret that sustains you in every moment / Michael Ray.
        p. cm.
    Includes bibliographical references and index.
    ISBN-10: 1-57675-286-0; ISBN-13: 978-1-57675-286-9 (alk pap.)
    ISBN-10: 1-57675-352-2; ISBN-13: 978-1-57675-352-1 (pbk.)
    1. Self-actualization (Psychology) 2. Goal (Psychology) I. Title.
BF637.S3R37 2004
158.1—dc 22   2004040973

First Edition 2004. First paperback edition 2005.
09 08 07   10 9 8 7 6 5 4 3 2

Interior Design: Laura Lind Design   Proofreader: Henrietta Bensussen
Copy Editor: Judith Brown   Indexer: Medea Minnich
Production: Linda Jupiter, Jupiter Productions

To my students and teachers:

May the flow of giving and receiving

continue without end.

This is the true joy of Life, the being used for a purpose recognized by yourself as a mighty one . . . the being a force of Nature instead of a feverish, selfish little clod of ailments and grievances complaining that the world will not devote itself to making you happy.

— G.B. Shaw, "Dedicatory Letter"
in *Man and Superman*

If not us, who?
If not here, where?
If not now, when?
If not for the kingdom, why?
Dare the dream.

— Anonymous,
adapted from Rabbi Hillel

Contentment is the highest goal.

— Chinese Proverb

Contents

Foreword

ON A WARM SEPTEMBER AFTERNOON IN 1982, I examined my assigned class schedule for the start of my second year in the Stanford MBA program. Mixed in with manufacturing strategy and corporate finance was a course simply titled Creativity in Business. "There's an oxymoron," I thought to myself. I'd added the course as an afterthought, to balance the rigors of my analytic curriculum.

At 3:20, I ambled into the seminar room, found a seat, and waited for class to begin. My classmates and I talked amongst ourselves, chatting about our summer job experiences and class schedules—waiting for the professors, Michael Ray and Rochelle Myers, to begin.

Nothing happened, so we chatted some more.

Still nothing happened.

Finally we noticed Michael and Rochelle sitting at the front of the room, waiting. The noise gradually died down, as each clump of chattering students noticed the teachers waiting patiently for us to turn our attention. Finally, Rochelle Myers—she couldn't have been more than five feet high, wearing a long flowing muumuu sort of thing with a giant silver medallion hanging down the front—stood up and said in a barely audible voice, almost a whisper: "You are about to embark on a ten-week journey to discover your deepest inner essence."

I immediately began flipping through the course catalogue for a replacement. My absorption in course listings was interrupted by Michael Ray starting us on a meditation exercise. "Breathe deeply, and slowly," said Michael. "Sense the energy in the toes of your right foot. Feel it begin to move through your foot. Concentrate on your right foot. Nothing to do but sense your right foot . . ." Somehow, it seemed to me, I'd made a very bad mistake.

That evening I told my wife Joanne that I had a great class schedule, "except for this one course that I'm going to drop." I told her about Rochelle and her muumuu thing, and about Michael—who reminded me of Yogi Bear in a rumpled professor's suit (only later did I discover that he really is a yogi, as in a spiritual guide)—leading us in meditation exercises. I'd majored in applied math in college. I'd worked at McKinsey. I had (and still have) a passionate love affair with data-driven analysis and research.

Joanne listened and then said simply, "I think that course might be really good for you. Why don't you stay in and just see what happens?"

What happened is simply this: I would not be where I am today, with the wonderful life I've been given, without that course. And I am not alone in this experience. Not a year goes by when I do not run into other graduates who feel just as I do, grateful that they had the course early in their lives. We did not know it at the time, but the experience would be the first step in a lifelong journey toward the topic of this book: finding and pursuing with courage and perseverance one's highest goal.

Still, the experience proved challenging for an insecure data geek. "When are we going to get some techniques for being creative, or management methods for making innovative products?" I challenged a couple of weeks into the course. I wanted tools, techniques, methods—something practical and useful.

Michael responded with the story of a businessman who visited a Zen master seeking enlightenment. They sat down for tea, the businessman blabbering on about all the issues and challenges in his life, and his quest for achievement and direction and meaning and purpose and . . . the master said nothing, pouring tea. With the cup full, the master kept pouring, the tea flowing into the saucer, onto the table, and finally into the man's lap.

"Hey! What are you doing?" yelped the businessman, leaping up as the scalding hot water seeped into his pants.

"Your cup is too full," said the master. "You add and add and add and add and add and add to your life. There is no room for enlightenment until you empty your cup."

Michael and Rochelle explained that this would not be a journey of adding skills and knowledge, but one of taking away barriers to creative potential. They operated from the premise that there is no such thing as an "uncreative person," but only those whose creativity is covered up. They endeavored to show us that we had a box of creative treasure in the attic, and all we had to do was a disciplined spring cleaning—tossing aside all the junk covering up the treasure box—so that we could open it up and look inside. The very point of it all lay in a fundamental challenge issued to each of us: *Make your life itself a creative work of art.*

In the years since, I've come to believe that there are two approaches to life. The first, followed by most, is the "paint by numbers kit" approach to life. You do what other people say. You follow a well-traveled path. You stay within the lines. And you end up with a nice, pretty—and unimaginative—picture. The second, followed by few, is to start with a blank canvas and try to paint a masterpiece. It is a riskier path, a harder path, a path filled with ambiguity and creative choice. But it is the only way to make your life itself a creative work of art. To paint a masterpiece requires a concept, a place to begin, a guiding context in the absence of the comforting numbers and lines in the premade kit. That guiding frame of reference is the highest goal, and bringing it into your life with the help of Michael's discoveries is what this book is all about.

When I took the creativity course in 1982, Professor Ray had not articulated the notion of the highest goal. Yet the idea was there all along, as an overarching framework, a hidden architecture for the entire creativity experience. Now, two decades later, Michael has identified and made visible that previously invisible meta-concept, and he brings it forth in these pages.

A core process—both in the course and in this book—is the idea of "live-with" heuristics. These are mantras of living that you implement for a period of time (usually a week or more), and reflect on the experience. At Stanford, we were challenged with such live-with assignments as: If at First You Don't Succeed, Surrender. Pay Attention! Ask Dumb Questions. Destroy Judgment, Create Curiosity. Don't Think About It. Be Ordinary. And the hardest live-with of all: Do Only What Is Easy, Effortless and Enjoyable. This last one came right at midterms and posed a problem: If I did only what was easy, effortless and enjoyable, I'd skip my midterm exams. So how could I fulfill the assignment in the creativity class without failing my other classes?

I decided to view midterms like the fourth pitch of the Naked Edge rock climb in Eldorado Canyon, Colorado. The Naked Edge has some of the most beautiful and spectacular climbing in all of North America; it is a perfect climb—except for the fourth pitch. Every time I climb the Naked Edge, I dread the fourth pitch. You have to climb up into an overhanging, downward flaring slot and wedge your body, like climbing up the inside of a bell—your feet slip and slide on the overhanging walls in the opening of the bell bottom, while your shoulders get all stuck and wedged in the tight upper cavity of the bell. It's an odd combination of claustrophobia and insecurity, made worse by the fact that none of the protection gear on the pitch is bomb-proof. (It's entirely possible if you fall out the bottom of the bell that some or all of the gear would pull out, and you'd take a long, perhaps bone-shattering fall.) Yet despite the fourth pitch, I've climbed the Naked Edge perhaps thirty times. Taken alone, the fourth pitch is just stress and drudgery. Taken in context of being in an amazing location on a beautiful day with a great comrade as a climbing partner, doing a sport that I love—well, the fourth pitch becomes part of an overall joyful day. I reframed midterms to be like the fourth pitch of the Naked Edge and sailed through with a much-improved frame of mind.

Michael's idea of the highest goal takes this idea to a much deeper level, a philosophical and spiritual answer to the question: What is your Naked Edge in life? What higher aspiration and purpose can you pursue with such passion that you can endure and gain strength for the stress and drudgery—the fourth pitch—required for the attainment of worthwhile and meaningful work?

The Highest Goal is the distillation of years of accumulated wisdom from a great teacher who has the humility to view his thousands of students as his teachers. What I most value about this book is its personal orientation. Professor Ray speaks directly to the individual, about what you can do to discover and follow your highest goal in life. It is a deeply subversive work; if you follow its teachings to their logical conclusion, you will almost certainly make significant changes in how you orient your life. In my own case, Michael and Rochelle challenged me in my mid-twenties to forgo the strictures of a traditional path, and to carve my own unique path in life. Their prodding set me on a path to find a happy, productive intersection between passion (what I love to do), genetic encoding (what I was put here on this earth to do) and economics (what I can make a living at). I discovered, in other words, the path to my highest goal. Perhaps, through the pages of this book, the same will happen for you.

Jim Collins

Boulder, Colorado

January 1, 2004

Preface

FOR A LONG TIME I have been hungering to share the secret of the highest goal with a broader audience. I've been on the trail of this discovery for several decades, distilling the essence of insights gleaned from twenty-five years of teaching the Personal Creativity in Business course at Stanford University.

The journey hasn't always been a direct one. The world has changed dramatically since I began teaching the course. It's become a more complex, chaotic and, in many ways, more dangerous place. At times I delved into other means of contributing to the growing movement toward a more humane and creative society. I searched for ways to help organizations transform into new paradigm businesses, to encourage people to make choices that would sustain the planet, to stimulate new approaches to leadership development, and to create networks and support systems for change.

Eventually I found that what was needed most was the work I was already doing. No one else seemed to be offering a way for each of us to bring our connection to our highest goal into our work, our organizations, our lives, and our world.

So about ten years ago, I dropped everything other than the creativity work. My colleagues and I continued to teach the creativity course at Stanford and other schools. Several of us also formed a company and developed software to offer the course to organizations and individuals outside of academia. We were astounded at the impact of the creativity work on people in businesses. Clients told us that the return on investment was at least one hundred and sometimes two hundred to one. That is, every one thousand dollars spent generated one hundred thousand to two hundred thousand in return.

But the benefits went beyond short-term financial results. People who hadn't spoken up or contributed much beyond their job descriptions started to blossom. Organization members who were about to leave decided to stay and contribute in a new way. Outstanding individuals joined the organization because it turned into the kind of workplace they wanted. It became a community—a community of individuals who welcomed all participants; thrived on diversity; fought gracefully; took the staff of leadership when necessary; and treated each other with compassion, acceptance, appreciation, and respect.

The Secret

What was going on here? Why was this course having this effect? Could I capture its essence so that it could be transmitted to more people? To answer these questions, I drew on my own and my colleagues' decades of experience teaching the course at Stanford and other schools, as well as the results from businesses and other organizations.

I found that the impact of the course went beyond its structure, procedures and exercises. It touched something very deep in people. They made discoveries about themselves that informed their actions and transformed their lives. Even though we never mention it in our teaching, they discovered their highest goal—the secret that would sustain them, come what may. As one participant put it years after taking the course, "This is transformation that works and lasts."

I recognized this same essential resource at work in other people who live creatively: They have a secret that centers them and makes their lives accomplished and fulfilling.

Many of the hundreds of guests we have welcomed to the creativity course are people who have discovered their highest goal. They are architects, artists, activists, war heroes, academics, singers, composers, dancers, entrepreneurs, engineers, scientists, financiers, psychologists, politicians, and monks. They have achieved enormous success by most standards, often amassing huge fortunes. Many have started new industries and changed the face of American and world culture. Still others have revolutionized the way we work and relate to others on an everyday basis.

When they visit the Personal Creativity in Business class, they talk about what got them where they are, and they describe their creative process and interior life. They share who they are at core and what they see as the purpose of their existence.

As I've listened to these people, and worked closely with thousands of students and participants, I've come to recognize the transforming power of the highest goal. When facing life's most trying tests, people rely on this secret to sustain them. When the world seems to be going crazy around them, these people are able to tap their inner resources, creatively serve others and bring their best to the world.

They learned—most early in their lives but many much later—through a crisis or through experiencing love and a connection to something higher that if they live for this connection, they keep growing closer to what is right for them. They are open to life and view it as an adventure. They don't get caught up in the exhortations of the media, the news of impending doom, the "shoulds" of their family and friends, or their own—often negative—mental meanderings.

Instead they see each situation and their potential role in it from a higher perspective. They take their time. They focus with intention. New possibilities open for them. They depend on a sort of grace that comes to them. They act creatively from this source.

This book focuses on this secret: your highest goal, something that is always there for you beyond the ordinary definitions of success.

A Radically Different Model of Success

When my colleagues and I developed Stanford's creativity course, we thought of it as a complement to other business courses. If our students could better access their creative side, we reasoned, that would help them leverage the analytical tools they were getting from virtually all the other courses in our school.

Eventually we realized, however, that these other courses actually promoted a way of life through the unspoken, fundamental assumption that economic success, together with its trappings, is the ultimate goal. The premise of our course was quite different: We wanted students to experience their inner wisdom and authority and the connection they had with all beings—another kind of success altogether. Without realizing it, we were not only offering a training program for a new way of doing business, but also of living in the world.

Students who discovered their essential inner resources and the ultimate purpose of their existence found they could do their work and live their lives in ways that contributed to positive change in the world. Alumni came back to tell us how they lived from that purpose and maintained their focus using the structure they had learned in our course. A few examples:

- Denise Brosseau built on her discovery in the course that, in essence, she is a connector. She cofounded the Forum for Women Entrepreneurs (FWE) soon after graduating from Stanford in 1993, changing the game for women entrepreneurs by helping them find funding and develop networks. For instance, one of her FWE conferences alone raised more than $185 million for twenty-six women-run start-ups.

- Jeff Skoll, who took the course in 1995, credits it with teaching him to look inside himself. He amassed a considerable fortune at eBay, earning a spot as one of the five richest people under forty in the United States. He then founded the Skoll Foundation, with the "mission of investing in, connecting and celebrating social entrepreneurs."

- Dominic Houlder, dean of the Sloan Program at the London Business School, has become quite prosperous both financially and in other ways in his career in business. He has also developed into a Buddhist teacher. In his recent book, *Mindfulness and Money: The Buddhist Path of Abundance*, he writes that this course "opened many students' eyes to spirituality in business . . ."[1]

When the course was offered to widows of victims of the 9/11 attacks, similar kinds of stories emerged. Though these women faced incredible life obstacles, the invocation of the highest goal is helping them take steps they never thought they could take. They inspire others to live lives that change the world for the better.

An Urgent Need

Society's fundamental assumptions too often lead to negative outcomes. We see the evidence in the growing gap between the haves and have-nots; increasing violence; endemic poverty and starvation; environmental degradation; the breakdown of values, integrity, communication, and community; a sense of unhappiness and fear; and poor health among people in even the richest nations.

Many of us feel an urgent need to change the status quo and contribute to a new positive direction. The world needs us all to contribute our best. But how can any individual affect what seems to be a massive concatenation of forces and, at the same time, face the challenges of his or her life?

This book answers that question. In this time of global transformation, we must act creatively and courageously from our deepest knowing and compassion. Only if we are living in service of the highest goal, in whatever way we experience it, can we meet the challenges of our times and fashion lives that work. And only if we discover ways of translating this highest goal into a new way of living, can it be practical and expansive for all.

Acknowledgments

In many of the world's spiritual traditions, the feminine provides the dynamic, creative aspect of life. So it is that aspect that I wish to humbly thank first. Women founded, created and sustained the course on which this book is based. Rochelle Myers put her wisdom, creativity and uncanny teaching ability into our course from the beginning. She planted the seeds that others of us have been nurturing all these years. Lorna Catford took up the torch left by Rochelle as she went on to simplify her life. Lorna started as a student of this material and then became a primary teacher and developer of it. Sandhya Abee brought many innovations into the course as we taught it together for several years and moved this material into a leadership class. Jackie McGrath (working in the early going with Sherri Lassila who designed our first company courses), perhaps more than anyone, helped to fashion the course in a way that it could be brought to thousands of people outside of academia.

Two women have brought the highest goal to my life and into the course through the years, even though they didn't participate in its teaching. Gurumayi Chidvilasananda has guided me with her teachings and nurtured the flame of my path from the time of my awakening in her tradition. By her grace I have experienced this course as my *seva*, my spiritual service.

Sarah Cecelia Ray, my life partner, brings the highest into my life and challenges me to live with it because of her clarity and lust for life. Everything in my life has changed since our first meeting over twenty-five years ago. She illustrates that love is the highest goal, and more specifically she set up a system and made sacrifices that made it possible for me to do the writing.

Others, male and female, have taught the course and taught me so much through the years—Stephen Miller, Steve Curtis, Hal Louchheim, Tom Kosnick, Todd Porter, John Vercelli, Pat Jordan, Jim Collins, Michelle Jurika, Françoise Netter, William Miller, Douglas Pressman, Fred Fischer, and all our Creativity in Business trained teachers—Athena Katsoras, Bruce Koren, Cheryl De Chantis, David Newman, Ginger Grant, John Davis, Julia Romaine, Julie Daley, Julie Saltonstall, Karin Albert, Kenton Hyatt, Lakiba Pittman, Martha Tilyard, Molly Fox, Pam Mayer, Paul Mlotok, Ron Nahser, Seema Khan, Sue Blondell, Tevis Trower, Theresa Leets, and Wayne Robertson—many of whose stories you'll find in this book. Their maturity, experience and energy are bringing this work to a new level that takes people to a life with the highest goal at an ever-faster pace. They give me faith in the future, and for that I am grateful.

Then there are the students and participants in our courses at Stanford and elsewhere. Some of them are mentioned in this book, but many are not. People like Steve Westly, Gary Marenzi, Michelle Barmazel, Stephen Phillips, Guillermina Castellanos, Shannon Williamson, Stephen Fields, Stephen Glikbarg, Larry Smith, Bob Moog, Gilberto Carrasquero, Charles Bresler, Lisa Phillips, Barry Sudbury, Jennifer Joss-Bradley, Brian Dowd, and Christopher Forman represent so many others who are not mentioned in this book but have taken the course and become my friends and teachers. It has been an honor and a gift to know them. Thank you also to Anne Durram Robinson, Lucia Marinelli, the late Father Peter Salmon, the Siddha Yoga swamis, Marilyn and Bill Veltrop and their Pathfinder Circles members, Patricia and Craig Neal and their Thought Leader Gatherings, FireHawk and Pele

Rouge, John Renesch and his Presidio Dialogues, and Father Mark Stetz for your inspiration.

This book wouldn't exist without the vision and guidance of my agent, Carol Roth, surely an author's best friend but also a yogi's best friend. And all the people at Berrett-Koehler were kind enough to make me part of their team and guide me and make this book a work of art (although I'm not too sure about the visual they picked for the cover). Steve Piersanti, Jeevan Sivasubramaniam, Rick Wilson, Michael Crowley, Ken Lupoff, Dianne Platner, Pat Anderson, and Robin Donovan took this project on when it was at a low point and made it into something completely new and exciting. And I'll never forget the great developmental editing by Chris Lee (her collaboration turned a manuscript into a book), the tough but illuminating early reviewing by Valerie Andrews, Joseph A. Webb, and Eileen Hammer, copyediting by Judith Brown, interior design by Laura Lind, proofreading by Henrietta Bensussen, indexing by Medea Minnich, and production administration by Linda Jupiter.

Finally, I thank my family, from my parents, Evelyn and Michael, my brother Dick and his family and all the Ray and Slavik relatives (some of whom are mentioned in this book specifically), to all of the people in Sarah's family who have welcomed me with such grace, to my six children and their families, including my eight grandchildren (the latest of whom, Eva Lucia Corral, is only a day old as I write this).

There is no way to thank you all sufficiently. You are the highest goal in living beings. May we be together again and again. May all be happy and living in the highest goal forever.

Introduction

MICHAEL BUSH LEANED on the edge of a table in front of one of our classes in Personal Creativity in Business at Stanford University and began to tell his story.

He started on a happy note. An alumnus of Stanford as well as the course, he is now president of Tetra Tech Wireless. Then he gave us a little background: After completing his master's degree, he became chief operating officer of a fast-growing high-technology firm. He is married and has two sons, and his wife is the chief technology officer of another company.

His company was a great place to work. It promoted high values and personal development for its employees. Company retreats featured outdoor events and generated an exciting atmosphere that supported trust, community and creativity. Word-of-mouth brought top talent to the door—people knew this was a great place to work.

Then the industry took a downturn. Michael's company lost business as more and more companies replaced its services with in-house departments. He was in trouble.

"I'd look into the mirror in the morning," he confesses, "and say to myself, 'You're going out of business!' Some nights I'd come home and my wife would know to keep the boys away from me."

He admits at times he despaired. When he was really low, he even cursed his courses at Stanford—including the one on personal creativity. But through it all, his sense of the highest goal would snap him back into focus.

He remembered that the highest goal for him translated into one word: Teacher. He got energy and felt a connection with something higher when he was teaching in the broadest sense. He knew that he could serve others if he drew on this strength. He knew that if he stayed in a giving, generative, collaborative role, he could navigate the worst situation and create a meaningful life.

Having profound faith in himself and his highest goal, he slowly turned things around.

He persevered through the stuff of COO nightmares. He took drastic measures, laying off ninety percent of the workforce. He rallied those who remained, and their values and high level of trust carried them through adversity. Inspired by his resolve, his people pulled together to reinvent the company.

Within a year the streamlined company began to grow as it served a completely different client base. Within two years, it was the industry leader, and its stock rose accordingly. Eventually the company merged with Tetra Tech, and Michael became the president of the resulting division.

Through it all, he stayed true to the principles of this book: He drew strength from his highest goal. He ended his talk to us by describing a full and well-rounded life. He goes home promptly for dinner virtually every night. He participates in community activities. He teaches in a nearby college in addition to his company duties. His wife continues in her CTO position at another company, but has negotiated a shorter workweek. Everyone in the family has grown as a result of the experience.

Of course, life will continue to happen. New challenges come up all the time. Even when, like Michael Bush, you know your highest goal and the best ways to move toward it, you must cope with life's surprises. None of the stories in this book are about living happily ever after. Instead, they are about living with more strength, perspective, peace and excitement.

Living with the Highest Goal

Michael Bush's story is not unique. People who live with the highest goal (even if they don't call it that) are able to weather the most difficult storms. In fact, they find themselves relying on this powerful resource as they navigate whatever challenges life tosses their way.

Lorna Catford not only took the creativity course but also became one of the main teachers and developers of it. She has lived with her highest goal for decades, and she recently found herself drawing strength from it in a very immediate way. When her doctor's office didn't let her know about the results of a test for cancer, she came face-to-face with fear. Her mind raced as she imagined the worst of scenarios, and then, something happened. But I'll let her tell the story:

> *Omigod. I'm going to die of cancer! No, it's just that they're disorganized in their office. No it isn't. They PROMISED they'd get back to me if it were OK. How will my family cope with me gone?*
>
> *On the way to work, I was writing my farewell letters in my head, planning the music I'd leave for my husband and kids, planning the music for my funeral. I knew about facing fear, and the more I faced the fear,*

the more I alternated between panic and doom. I knew about moving towards pleasure. What pleasure when your days are so numbered? I knew about finding a gift in all of this. Right. Joke of the century.

Then something happened.

As I drove down the highway, the fields and even other cars seemed beautiful, filled with a sort of spiritual glow. I felt at peace. Parking in the far-away parking lot, as is my habit, and walking across campus to my office, I breathed in the beauty of the grass, the trees, the million-colored flowers, the million-colored leaves. In class and in meetings, I was ON. Electricity, or maybe energy, was present in everything and every interaction—from the ridiculousness of a malfunctioning computer saga to the inspiration of students in class.

Somehow, I'd come to the place of walking through the fear, although I sort of did it blindfolded, or backwards, without realizing it.

When I arrived home there was a message from the doctor saying everything looked fine. Phew. This was enough of a test for me, though.

And the gift? The proof positive that even in the face of a "worst fear," spirit comes through.

Often a crisis, such as Michael's troubles with his company or Lorna's health scare, gives people a sense of their highest goal. It enables them to survive crises and turn them into breakthroughs in business and elsewhere in their lives.

What Is the Highest Goal?

So what *is* this Highest Goal? What is it like to experience, and how can it revolutionize your life?

Many philosophical traditions tell us that we have within us amazing potentiality, including that of the whole universe. In one tradition, the saints and sages talk about experiencing this potential as a tiny, shimmering blue pearl of light. They tell us that they gaze at the blue pearl, and it fills their body or it explodes to reveal the universe.

Eastern nonsense? Well, consider that as Western science catches up to this kind of "nonsense," it has discovered that the power of many nuclear reactions is present in even a cubic centimeter of empty space—if only it could be utilized.

The highest goal is simply to be in this experience of connection or truth (no matter how you refer to it) all the time. That remains a goal, of course, because this is something you spend a lifetime working toward rather than attaining. But your commitment motivates, inspires and guides your journey, and gives you more and more time in this state of connection.

If you live for the highest goal, you are living a life of the spirit—whether or not you consider yourself to be on a spiritual path. If you consciously notice the larger aspects of life, always consider whether what you are doing coincides with these aspects, never forget the times when you were enlivened by the power of the highest goal, use those memories in new situations, and act with the knowledge of the support you have and the journey you are on—you will be living for the highest goal.

As one spiritual teacher put it, "On this globe there is almost endless diversity. Nevertheless, the greater fact is that when it comes to the treasures of the soul, differences vanish. In the place of the heart, only one light shines. This light is the same in all beings. Unveiling the Truth, becoming established in the experience of this light, is the goal of spiritual pursuit."

Similarly, this spiritual pursuit takes many different forms, but the paths all lead to the highest goal. The great choreographer, Twyla Tharp, spoke of it when she said, "I work for God. Me and God."[1]

Bob Landouceur, a high school football coach who has led his team to more than one hundred and forty straight wins over a dozen seasons (perhaps the longest winning streak in sports at any level), says it another way: "If a team has no soul, you're just wasting your time."[2] Every week he attempts to get his players to strengthen the bonds of community and openly speak of the love they feel.

"This is his ultimate goal every season," observes *Fast Company* magazine in an article about Landouceur's approach to the game. "His winning streak is a national obsession, but keeping it going seems to mean less to him than getting 45 boys to say the L word out loud."[3]

What's It to You?

Stories about other people achieving and overcoming odds may be inspirational, but until you consciously experience how you are supported by your own connection to the highest goal, it is difficult to comprehend and make a part of your life.

So take a few minutes right now to think about, contemplate and even relive a situation in which you experienced resonance with the highest goal. Concentrate on one of these situations, whether it happened recently or a long time ago.

The situation you pick can be simple, even commonplace. You can experience the highest goal when you look into the face of a newborn baby (particularly if it is your baby), when you hit a perfect golf or tennis shot, or say just the right thing in a meeting or to a friend. You get this kind of rush of energy and peace when you execute a series of perfect dance steps, get absorbed in a sunset, experience love for someone, or feel at one with the water while swimming.

You connect with your highest goal when you awaken full of enthusiasm for the day and when you know you are making a contribution. It is synonymous with being in the flow, —periods in which you are so totally absorbed with what you are doing that time stops and fulfillment comes naturally. It is making your life itself a work of art. It is working at something that you're getting paid to do that you would secretly be willing to pay someone to be able to do.

It is the experience you have when you first fall in love. Problems at work don't seem to be such problems anymore. You can handle them. You can work productively with people you may have considered enemies. You see their goodness underneath the tough exterior. You're in love. Everything looks, feels, *is* different.

This kind of resonance is catalytic. Similar to a chemical catalyst, which causes reactions without being diminished, it is endlessly generative. Once you realize that it has been there for you a number of times in your life, you begin to see the enormity of it. You see that you are operating in a world in which you can draw on grace. Once you see that possibility, you can begin to act with intention relative to the highest goal and better align your efforts with this generative process.

The Most Meaningful Thing

Do you have a situation in mind? You may find it hard to put your experience into words. Resonance with the highest goal has that overwhelming power that the scientists tell us about, that the sages see as the dazzling blue pearl, that your own experience validates. But how can you talk of its enormity?

You can start on this journey of noticing your times of connection by using the following series of questions to help you go deeper. Once you have tried this several times, you can begin to get into a beneficial habit of acknowledging your inner greatness and enjoying its various aspects.

You might find it helpful to take some notes as part of this exercise; yet know that you can do it in your head without any writing if that is more convenient for you.

First, recall the most meaningful thing you did in the last week or so. It could be something similar to the situation you just recalled, but think of something that happened recently. Whatever it is, re-experience doing that activity. See it in your mind's eye and get the feeling of what made this activity so meaningful. (Notice that I am not asking you to recall some earthshaking event or accomplishment, just the activity that was most meaningful in the last week or so.) You may want to jot down a few notes about this situation just to identify it for yourself.

Second, answer the question, "How come this was so important, so meaningful to me?"

Then answer the question, "Why is that (the reason you gave to the previous question) so important to me?"

And keep asking the question, "Why is that so important to me?" of every answer you give until you get down to one word.

That word, if you dig below possible negative reasons (such as fear) or external reasons (such as money) that you have for doing something, represents just one quality of your essence, your Self. When you see what that word is—be it Love, Communication, Wisdom, Energy, Tranquility, Fun, Creativity, Service, Silence, Connection, Peace, Joy, or any number of other qualities that may be part of who you are at core—acknowledge that quality as being part of who you really are. Remember it. Revel in it. Contemplate it. See how it has been a guiding quality in your life. Notice it coming up as you deal with each new situation.

When I ask a group of people to do this Most Meaningful Thing exercise together, we shout out our words at the same time. Then we make time for individuals to say their personal words that came from the exercise. We are moved by the depth of these words as qualities of who we are. Eventually we get the truth that all these words are part of who we are, although they have different meanings for each of us.

If you look at the various words that surface as you use this exercise for any activity, you can see how you can move more quickly to faith and flow in your life. For instance, one man who did this exercise talked about visiting and taking care of his aged and ill father. He first wrote about fear as a reason that he did the activity. He was afraid that if he didn't take care of his dad, he would not be seen as a good son. But then as he worked through the exercise, he realized successively that Connection, Creativity, Joy, Love, and, finally, Peace were underlying the meaningfulness of this activity.

Outer responsibility and fear initially moved him to act, yet the activity became meaningful because of deep traits that were part of his Self. Peace was the highest goal for him. He kept working with this realization with each visit, until his faith propelled him to an experience of genuine Peace with his father. Even though there were difficulties in their relationship, out of this came a flow of compassion and energy that made their last days together complete, an experience of the highest goal for each of them.

What Is Your Highest Goal?

You can use the Most Meaningful Thing exercise to get an idea of the highest goal for you. Review your most meaningful activity and the process you used to get to the one word. Look at that one word as a quality that represents you at core. Consider how that quality has operated in your life. See how often it has figured in your various experiences of the highest goal that you may have contemplated earlier in this chapter. Remember crises and turning points in your life, and see how this quality figured in these events. Savor what your life is like when you are living from this quality.

Remember, it is ultimately an experience of resonance with a larger energy. Though people express it in different ways—connecting with God, merging with the absolute, being in flow with the Tao, enlightenment, doing God's work, being a channel for love and compassion, being conscious at all times, and finding and living from one's Self—they are talking about the same thing. The highest goal is to have this experience all the time, to become established in it.

Essentially, I'm asking you to state the highest goal in your own words, which might be different from the examples I've given here.

Are you ready to make an initial statement of the highest goal for you? Remember, you'll be exploring your understanding of the highest goal throughout this book and your life. Here, just see what comes up.

Please complete the following sentence:

The highest goal for me is _____

_____

_____

_____.

Once you've written this statement or thought about it, you might share your understanding with someone who has done the same thing. Notice how your statements, however different, are ultimately based on experience that connects them at a deeper level. There might be some nervous laughter and joking about this, because you are thinking and talking about a great, almost transcendent purpose for your life, and this conversation can be uncomfortable at times.

But these conversations usually produce insights into the highest goal. For instance, Steve Piersanti, founder and CEO of Berrett-Koehler Publishing, originally thought his highest goal was the same as his personal and business purpose: "Making a World that Works for All." But when he did the Most Meaningful Thing exercise, he came up with the word or quality Family. He saw that his highest moments came when he experienced that everyone was part of the same human family. This highest goal sustained him as he built his business around his purpose and as he faced challenges in all parts of his life. I believe Steve's highest goal led to the diverse, creative and compassionate community that makes up his publishing team, and that makes it possible for his purpose to be realized.

John Renesch, an entrepreneur who became an author of many books (for example, *Getting to the Better Future*), publisher, keynote speaker, founder of the Presidio Dialogues, and social observer and philosopher, felt quite clearly that his calling was to help people negotiate the jolting paradigm shift in the world of work with exultation rather than misery. He talks about how this has always been his purpose, even before he knew it, even in his entrepreneurial days. But when he did the Most Meaningful Thing exercise, he distilled his experience down to the word Trust. He realized that his trust in God helped him through difficult business and personal times, and supported him in his calling. When he experienced that, he saw that living with that highest goal was the foundation for his work.

I have done the Most Meaningful Thing exercise dozens of times, and the word or quality that comes up for me is some version of Communion (Communication, Connection, Compassion or Community). My work is helping people to live from their inner resources in order to create a world that works for everyone, a world in which people can see themselves and each other with their hearts, a world based on Truth and Love. But the highest goal that underlies that purpose is Communion, that sense of unity and flow that I get when I am living and moving toward the highest goal for me. It helps me see problems as opportunities.

Discoveries to Use on Your Journey

What about you? Do you see the nature of the highest goal for your life? As you contemplate this question, you may want to jot down a few thoughts. Make this a continuing process of understanding. As you read this book and bring its ideas into your life, you'll get a better sense of your own quest and touchstone. Let your statement that you put into words earlier be the start of your commitment to live from the highest goal.

Know that this is a journey; only a few of us achieve the highest goal fully in our lifetime. Yet you can integrate the journey to the highest goal into your everyday life, bring out your best as you face challenges and bring harmony and energy into every moment.

Once you commit to living with the highest goal, certain steps will help you on your way. These steps are the discoveries I've made in the Stanford creativity work. If you practice any of these steps, you'll be ahead of the game. Do them all and your life will be changed for the better forever.

1. **Go beyond passion and success.** Living for the highest goal is radically different from what is normally considered the highest: reaching success in external terms and having passion for what you do in life. Most of us "sub-optimize," that is, we go for the short-term and transitory. Go beyond these lesser goals to use the gift of life you have been given.

2. **Travel your own path.** You can create your own
   path by simply paying attention to your own best
   performance—the critical incidents in your life—
   when you feel most your Self, in flow and in tune
   with the highest goal. Remember the experience of
   these times, apply what works to new situations and
   keep improving your path to the highest goal.

3. **Live with the highest goal.** Because everything in
   the world is a connected system, you can't beat it,
   you can only join it. And the best way of joining it is
   to live with heuristics—generalizations or rules of
   thumb for learning and discovery. Without this practice of living with heuristics—such as Pay Attention,
   Ask Dumb Questions, See with Your Heart, or Be
   Ordinary, or other "live-withs"—the content of this
   book remains just that, content. Enliven your journey with live-withs.

4. **Find true prosperity.** The more you express and experience your highest qualities, the more you are filled
   with a rich feeling of self-worth, and the wealthier you
   will become in the truest sense. Find the prosperity
   that will sustain you through the ups and downs of life
   and keep increasing, even through difficulties.

5. **Turn fears into breakthroughs.** When you have the
   grounding of the highest goal, you can see your fears
   for what they are. Learn from them, and turn their
   energy into breakthroughs and opportunities of the
   most lasting kind.

6. **Relate from your heart.** I define "compassion" as seeing the highest in your Self first and then seeing the highest in others. If you have a full, rich feeling of self-worth, you have already taken the first step toward having compassion. See others from this perspective, and you begin to change the nature of your relationships for the better and make connections that move you toward the highest goal.

7. **Experience synergy in every moment.** You can achieve synergy—a much more dynamic state than balance—among the parts of your life by developing organizing structures based on your highest goal and by getting into the flow of intuitive decision-making.

8. **Become a generative leader.** Generative leaders pass along their experience of the highest goal and ignite creativity in others. Share the fruits of your quest for the highest goal with others, and spread its effect in a beneficial spiral.

The rest of this book is devoted to these steps. In a sense, once you know your highest goal and these eight discoveries, you know everything that is in this book. But unless you live with the highest goal and interact fully with these discoveries, you will have only knowledge. Use them, and you will go beyond knowledge to live with wisdom—the wisdom that comes from within you and beyond you and that sustains you in your life's journey.

Go Beyond Passion and Success

ALMOST WITHOUT FAIL, when I ask people to tell me their highest goal, they give me what a company would call a purpose, a part of its organizational vision. People are often magnanimous, saying they exist to improve the lot of others, to leave the world a better place or simply to serve. Sometimes they refer to their own personal development. One person, for example, told me her highest goal was to adapt.

If I keep asking the question in different ways—"That's good, but what goal do you have that supports you in living out that purpose?" or "What allowed you to get past that difficult time that you had last year?"—most people eventually begin to get at their highest goal.

Few people say their highest goal is something material—the very nature of the question goes deeper than a desire to win the lottery or own a beach house. Still, very few people talk about the highest goal that probably has been with them from the beginning of their life and that has been supporting them in everything they do.

I suspect that is because we are conditioned to talk about our highest goal in terms of our potential contribution, rather than about the force that helps us to make that contribution.

Your Early Experience of the Highest Goal

Researchers tell us that all of us have a defining experience of the highest goal early in our lives, usually around the time of puberty. We each have an experience that we are great, that we have a connection with everything, that we have potential. That is the moment of exultation captured by Walt Whitman's "Song of Myself":

> *I celebrate myself, and sing myself,*
> *And what I assume you shall assume,*
> *For every atom belonging to me as good belongs to you.*

This experience, if we accept it and remember it, can catapult us beyond the socialization and comparisons that deter us from living the purpose of our lives. This experience, this earliest awareness of the highest goal, can be the starting point for living with a conscious connection to it.

A friend of mine shared an experience that this illustrates: When she was about eleven, her family was on a tour of Italy. One day they were visiting the St. Paul's Outside the Walls Church in Rome. She was a bored kid, who, in her opinion, had been through too many churches on the trip. But as she went into a side chapel dedicated to Mary Magdalene, she experienced energy and a feeling of connection that she remembers to this day. Curiously, she didn't tell anyone about this until later in her life when she happened to be talking to a scholar of Mary. That conversation opened her to a consciousness that was her highest goal and that she could see had been part of her life since that day in Rome.

I urge you now to remember and contemplate a time when you experienced the nature of your highest goal. You have had such an experience, maybe more than once. Do you remember it? Push yourself a little here, because it is worth it. Recall a time, probably in your early life, when you had an epiphany about your own potential, about who you really are in a powerfully positive sense, about your connection to all beings and all nature.

Perhaps I'm using words that don't quite fit for you. Remember I'm talking about the experience of the highest goal itself, which is personal and diverse. Some people get a sense of themselves and this connection when they see something in nature, such as mountains or an ocean, for the first time. Sometimes they have this deep feeling about who they really are in a religious setting, in a sports competition, as the result of a powerful dream, or after great exertion. But often it's simply a gift that is given to us early in our lives. It just happens when we least expect it.

Once you start thinking about it, you may be able to think of several times when you have had such an experience. Concentrate on the earliest, most powerful one you can remember. Look beyond the nature of your experience to focus on what it told you about the highest goal. Please take some time to reflect on it, jot some notes about it and/or talk to someone about it. If you can resurrect this memory and nurture it in terms of your own highest goal, you have something extremely valuable for the journey we are taking in this book.

I remember walking barefoot along a gravel road in Wisconsin. I was ten years old. It was a beautiful summer day, and I was walking toward a beach on a lake. I recall this sensation of connection with everything. I experienced the whole—from the bright sun, vast blue sky and tall trees to the pebbles under my feet and the grasshoppers leaping up as I walked forward—as being part of me. I felt huge. I knew that I was put on earth to do something great. I also felt a sense of sadness because this life would have to end sometime. I began to get a sense of change and the flow of great forces that I was a part of. All this happened in moments, but the experience was powerful and touched every part of my being.

Of course, I put aside that experience as society kept telling me what to do and who I was. Just like my friend who felt the highest goal as a connection to Mary Magdalene, I didn't talk to anybody about what had happened. But I remember it now.

Most people seem to forget the memory of their early connection to the highest goal, but the memory is still there. You only need to concentrate to bring it up. A great many people have told me about recapturing this memory: One fellow remembered his father telling the young boy forcefully that he was great. A woman recalled helping with the birth of a calf on her aunt's farm, and afterward she got a sense of the meaning of her life. Still another slipped out of her home early in the morning when she was two and a half years old. She walked into an Episcopal Church down the block, and she discovered, as she put it, "the existence of grace."

After a seminar in which I urged people to remember their childhood moments, a woman came up to tell me she remembered a time walking in the mountains when she was an adolescent. She suddenly felt the connection and energy I am talking about. In her case, it gave her a sense of the control she had in a difficult family situation. She said that unlike her older sister, who was tormented end-lessly by their parents and ended up embittered by her childhood, she was able to make choices that kept her free. To this day, she goes to the mountains for renewal and always remembers the power she has. It has helped her deal with stress and problems with relationships, as well as take advantage of opportunities that present themselves.

What happened to you? Do you remember an experience of connection? If so, don't forget it now.

Obstacles to Grace I: Sub-Optimizing

Most people forget their youthful experience of greatness and pur-pose or at least put it aside somewhere deep in their memory. It hap-pens to all of us: We sub-optimize.

By sub-optimizing I mean that we may have an experience of the highest goal in our lives, but we quickly pull back to the lesser goals that society calls success. We often get frozen in our accom-plishments, which may be great, but not the highest or optimal that we can attain. In other words, we settle; we sub-optimize.

In every moment we have a choice: Will we act from our highest goal or recede to something less? For instance, sometimes in meetings I speak my truth no matter what the consequences for me. On other occasions I pull back to a comfortable silence and miss chances to make a real contribution. When the latter occurs, I always feel sad, but I try to learn from it.

Sometimes we keep doing the same thing that brought us success in society's terms. When this happens early in a career, I call it the tragedy of early success. Some people—athletes, entertainers, entrepreneurs, artists, writers, and scientists, for example—have tremendous success early in their careers. The media lionize them, and these initially successful people keep trying to do the same thing over again. But they can never get beyond that early success. They develop no further and sub-optimize their lives. It is something that can happen to all of us.

Obstacles to Grace II: The Cruel Grip of Socialization and Comparison

Of course, the most powerful obstacles to living in resonance with the highest goal come from the media, our schools, our parents and friends—our society. All of them tell us to chase a successful life that will be admired by others.

That influence invades our dreams and our deepest thoughts. It holds us with a cruel grip. We buy into the game that society convinces us we should be playing, even if it draws us away from who we are at core. We miss some of our greatest moments. We rationalize them away. We can't put them together into a consistent way of living our lives because we allow ourselves to be distracted by the picture of success and the good life that these forces of society offer us.

We constantly compare ourselves with others. And when we do this, we lose control of our lives because we are no longer living from our core. We are living according to someone else's idea of what life should be or what we should be doing. We lose the power that comes from doing what is right for us.

Beyond Passion and Success

Over and over my students tell me that they yearn to have passion in their work, but they just don't know how to find it. This must be true for many people, because books on finding your purpose and bringing it out into the world seem to proliferate in bookstores everywhere. Still, people complain they haven't been able to find their passion the way others have.

I trace the difficulty and anguish to the human propensity to make comparisons. Instead of diving into who they are and what that means for their work, people look to those who seem to be successful and seem to have passion in their lives. Instead of discovering how they resonate with the highest goal and applying that to their life, they put themselves down and sink into frustration when their life isn't the way others' lives seem to be.

Once I got so tired of hearing this wail about lack of passion that I told my class that it was overrated. I thought I would give them some peace because they wouldn't have to keep worrying about other people who had the passion that they didn't. They could just concentrate on themselves and what was really happening in their lives. They could begin to build on their own experiences.

But my "magnanimous" gesture didn't seem to help. They filled their papers and presentations with diatribes on the importance of passion. They told me in many ways that I had let them down. Like all of us, these students desperately wanted something in their lives, but they didn't know how to get it.

The students' angst about passion represents something we all feel, particularly when we act in accordance with the way we have been socialized to act rather than from what is right for us. We get our dream job and then find out it just doesn't give us fulfillment. We take a class or enter a course of study that we think is sure to give us what we need to be a success and find that it has just brought us new questions about what we want to do with our life. We don't get as much pleasure doing the things that we have staked our lives on. We get excited about something for a while, but then it becomes humdrum and doesn't give us sufficient reason to get out of bed. We feel inferior when we see other people who seem to have such energy for life, while we wake up too many mornings without any zest. Or, even worse, we start thinking that life has passed us by, that it is meaningless, and that we'll never make the contribution or have the life we imagined when we were younger.

Taking Your Own Path

The alternative is so close at hand: If we focus on our highest goal, our passion comes to us effortlessly. We know at some deep level that we have a distinctive contribution to make. But, as Carl Jung said, we make the mistake of going outside to find direction:

> Your vision will become clear only when you look into your heart. Who looks outside, dreams. Who looks within, awakens.[1]

The highest goal is part of the human quest. Eastern traditions call life purpose "dharma," or right livelihood. India's *The Bhagavad-Gita,* for example, focuses almost entirely on dharma and the search for it. In it Lord Krishna says to his pupil Arjuna, "Better one's own dharma, however imperfect, than the dharma of another perfectly performed."

In this society we almost never follow Krishna's advice. Too often, our parents, teachers and the media train us to define happiness in terms of external rewards.

We take one of the two paths in life shown in the figure below. Doing someone else's dharma well starts when you do what society says to do, even though it is not something you like. Over time, you get experience with it and get good at it. So you get opportunities to do more of this work. You get promoted. You become the boss, the partner or a top executive. Everyone honors you and wants you to do more of something that isn't right for you. And you experience your life getting more and more meaningless and unsatisfying.

The path of doing your own dharma starts with doing what you love and what is meaningful to you. In time you gain both experience and skill. You get very good at it. And, because of that, you get more opportunity to do the kind of work that represents who you really are. Even though you might get the trappings of success— money, fame, promotions, and awards—the work itself remains its own reward. Your life keeps getting more and more fulfilling. And

TWO ALTERNATIVE LIFE PATHS

Do what you don't like, but should	Do what you love and find meaningful
Get experience doing this	Get experience doing what you love
Become great at doing what you dislike	Become extra good at you doing what you love
Gain opportunity to do more	Gain more opportunity to do what you love.
Live life empty of meaning	Live life full of purpose and meaning

your satisfaction gives blessings to your friends, family, community and the world.

Mahatma Gandhi taught that only service done with joy can have meaning. Here, I'm calling this joy a resonance with the highest goal. If you have that, your service will have meaning beyond what you can imagine. Specifically, Gandhi said

> Service can have no meaning, unless one takes pleasure in it . . .
>
> Service which is rendered without joy helps neither the servant nor the served.
>
> But all other pleasures and possessions pale into nothingness before service that is rendered in the spirit of joy.[2]

Remembering Your Own Highest Goal

Sometimes this idea of the two possible paths in life upsets people. Students who have already accepted jobs that they know are not fulfilling wonder if they have made an unalterable error. People who are already working at something that doesn't give them joy and meaning can wonder if it is too late to do anything about it. Yet even when they want to go in a new direction, they don't know their highest goal, so they feel lost.

All of this confusion comes from not holding onto your own highest goal. We all glimpse it from time to time, but only if we are attentive to this guiding star when it appears can we steer by it. I know this from my own experience.

When I was twenty, I wasn't used to doing much on my own. I had done well as a student. But I was treated by my family as something of an idiot savant—bright in school, but unable to deal with the real world. I believed what my family told me. I accepted their guidance and handling of worldly affairs.

Then I was faced with helping friends, a couple, out of crisis. She was pregnant, and they wanted to get married before they told their parents. None of the three of us were yet the legal age of twenty-one, but they asked me to make arrangements for them. I was on my own; I couldn't depend on my parents or older brother this time.

I called government agencies and people who might perform the ceremony. I was nervous and unsure of myself, but I noticed that once I got on the calls, I was very resourceful. I came up with alternatives, I made suggestions, I let no difficulty stand. I just kept going. And everything worked out.

We drove to another state, and I stood up for them with the woman's sister at the little ceremony. That incident altered my perception of what was possible—both for me and for the world. It opened me to the resources that are always there for us.

Of course, I quickly reverted back to shyness and concentrating on what seemed most important to me: eking out a career in the context of what society and my family thought was appropriate—not what my greatest possibility and contribution might be—often acting out of feelings of alienation, anxiety and anger. But something about that experience stayed with me. Every once in a while I had to step up to a challenge that I hadn't faced before (which happened frequently after I myself got married and took on responsibilities as husband and father). I realized that the same resources available to me earlier were available in these other situations. The more I drew upon my larger inner resources, the easier it became to use them in new situations.

I didn't know it, but I was building the basis for the career I have now—helping people to live from their inner resources all the time and in all situations. At the same time, I was relating more and more to the highest goal for me. I've learned that the more people can live this way, the more they begin to love and respect themselves and the people around them. They can serve in a meaningful way. They can grow in the most difficult of situations.

How the Highest Goal Pursues You

What about you? Have you remembered an instance in your life that defined the highest goal for you? How would you characterize the highest goal for yourself right now?

Even if you can't remember such an experience, take comfort in knowing that this highest goal pursues you. In fact, when you experience discomfort and aimlessness in your life, you are resisting the pull to live for the highest goal. But if you keep at it and don't get distracted, the difficulty will draw the highest goal into your life.

I've seen that movement from difficulty to insight and new movement over and over again with the famous and not-so-famous people I have worked with. The highest goal will give direction, especially when times are tough. I'm not talking about anything mystical here. I'm talking about a natural process that occurs if you are forced to draw upon your inner resources. Something clicks in. You draw upon resources that you didn't know you had. You have experiences that remind you of your highest goal. And, for a period of time, you are in resonance with it.

I know because I've experienced this cycle myself. I went through a time when my career and business were going well, but personally I was lost. Even though I had experienced a resonance with the highest goal, I slid into feeling very low and close to depression. After a great deal of work on myself, pushed on me by this difficult time, I experienced an awakening, a new sense of the highest goal. It happened quite unexpectedly.

I attended a meditation-intensive day at an ashram to support a friend. As I sat in meditation in what was for me an unfamiliar environment, I suddenly felt and saw a bolt of lightning shoot up from the base of my spine out the top of my head. It forced me to recognize something great within me. And that recognition led to an experience of joy unlike anything I had ever had before. I was whole. I was full of love. The problems I had been having and the low opinion I had of myself seemed miniscule in relation to this awareness of my own divinity. I had been taking courses that were enormously useful in getting me to this point, but now I was shifting beyond anything these courses could have hoped to give me.

For some reason, perhaps my sense of masculinity at the time, I tried to stop crying for joy and my throat hurt with the effort. But I couldn't stop it, and tears of joy flowed without restraint. Then my legs started to vibrate and shake. Their shaking caused me to bounce on the floor in an almost involuntary way. Then I became still and went into a black void that seemed to be all of existence. I sat there for a long time in that state until the end of the meditation session.

I see now that everything that has evolved in my life in the last twenty-seven years since that moment of awakening came from that insight into the highest goal. I understood in that instant that there is a reason and foundation for everything that happens. Because of that experience I was able to see the other clues to my connection to the highest goal that I've mentioned.

And I understand now that I really don't do anything. I just stay tuned to that connection with what is transcendent in the world. If I keep at it, exactly what is supposed to happen takes place.

Just as a composer or artist gets an insight and then spends years implementing that insight, I have been working through the result of that awakening experience in my life. I have been discovering ways that all of us can recognize the awakenings in our lives and apply them to the business of living.

Travel Your Own Path

WHAT DOES THE HIGHEST GOAL mean to you right now? Is it an unattainable myth? A worthy support? Something that helps you on your journey through life? Something that sounds good, but should be avoided because it is reserved for a select few?

Consider the words of Sakyong Mipham, a Tibetan Buddhist and author of *Turning the Mind into an Ally.* When he was asked whether enlightenment is a goal or a process, he answered, "I think enlightenment is our nature."[1]

It is your nature, too. The process of finding your way to the highest goal, which Mipham calls enlightenment, is what makes your journey through life meaningful. In a sense, as Mipham teaches, you already have enlightenment. And as you travel your path, you will find your own way to the highest goal.

Creating Your Own Way

The necessity of finding and following your own way is the stuff of timeless legend and lore. In the stories of King Arthur and his roundtable, for example, the magician Merlin brings each knight to a part of the forest where there is no path so that each will be forced to find his own.

We often avoid the quest for the highest goal because it is frightening to create our own way. We allow ourselves to be diverted by the thousand things that pull at us every day—work, family responsibilities, entertainment—or we settle for someone else's path. Even those of us who practice a particular religion or spiritual tradition must bring it into our lives in our own way, or it will never be meaningful for us beyond agreeable theory or pleasant ritual.

Early in life, most of us borrowed a path from others, primarily from our parents or some tradition. People around us give us models. In my life, for instance, my mother gave me the model of openness to others, my father of communication, attention to detail and going slowly at first as you learn something new. My Aunt Bess passed on to me the power of gratitude. Through his writing, the great golfer and coach Tommy Armour introduced me to the idea of paying attention to my best performance and traits and ignoring bad habits—a core suggestion of this book. Many other people, some of whom I didn't even know, showed me models for all kinds of situations.

We all use these early directions, at least for a time. Consider the creative history of great artists such as Picasso or Beethoven. Their early work is technically outstanding and promising, but derivative. Eventually, they began to strike out on their own and create new approaches. Picasso developed cubism, and Beethoven created the remarkable transcendence in his Late Quartets. The work of both artists is so distinctive that you don't have to be told whose work it is—you just know.

Other artists who are not as well known also develop distinctive styles, achieve a life of fulfillment and make a contribution. But many others fail to find their own way, and they miss the opportunity to move to the highest goal.

The key is to pay attention to what works for you so that you begin to develop your own path. You don't reject the people and traditions of your early life; rather, you begin to develop your own tradition and work with your own teachers.

This is a lifelong journey—no matter how old you are, this process of finding what works and discovering your path gives your life meaning. You continually develop your understanding of your relationship to the highest goal. By creating from your highest goal and living on your path toward it, you inspire others. And this becomes your greatest legacy.

A Conscious Life

When I think of people who forge their own path, I often think of my late friend Tom Siporin. In the middle of his life, he began to follow a particular spiritual tradition with a highest goal of realization. He developed his own way of traveling with this highest goal, living every moment with compassion's slogan, "I am." It was his way of keeping the highest goal in mind no matter what.

Tom's path seemed to be littered with obstacles. He contracted polio as a child and was left with one normal and one tiny, withered arm. But he became a star one-armed pitcher in high school and lettered in baseball and soccer at Harvard. He graduated cum laude and went on to become a lawyer, championing the disabled and underprivileged, always loving to play and win at baseball, tennis, Ping-Pong, and basketball.

Then bone cancer attacked his body, and after he had a leg amputated, he decided to spend the end of his life pursuing his creative abilities. He produced enough art for over forty exhibitions, wrote books of ecstatic poetry, and lyrics and books for a half dozen musical comedies. At the same time, he enriched his community and used his legal skills to help those less fortunate.

After his death at age fifty-nine, friends and relatives attending his memorial were lavish in expressing the love they felt for him. Everyone found it hard to represent the joy of being with him, and the integrity and absolute trust he exuded. But they noted, also with love, that he could be stubborn when it came to artistic questions. Jessica Bryan, founder and director of the New Theater Company that produced a number of Tom's plays, said that she never had public shouting matches with anyone other than Tom. But that conflict produced wonderful creative work, she said.

Tom exemplified the power of the highest goal that you also have within yourself, in your own way. He overcame incredible obstacles to manifest his potential for the good of all. He exuded dignity and yet absolutely bubbled with childlike abandon and fun. I never saw him shirk from telling the truth, as he knew it, even if it was difficult to tell. He saw the highest in others and so brought out the best in everyone around him.

Tom still gives me a new perspective when I need one. If he were still alive, I suspect he would respond to the current state of the world by writing musical comedies that would skewer the demagogues and pundits, point out the real issues underlying the confusion and bias in the media, and, in general, make light of our anxiety by putting everything in a larger context. Just thinking about him, I hear his booming voice, and he helps me link to the highest goal, no matter what situation I'm in. And I know I'm not the only friend of Tom's who still finds inspiration in him and his quest.

The Crucible of Your Living Legacy

Have you noticed what happens to people like Tom when they face overwhelming obstacles? They live with such gusto that they are an inspiration. Why do some people seem to overcome tragedy, while others are destroyed by it?

Consider the possibility that crisis, tragedy or enormous life obstacles push people like Tom to live from their highest expression and see their challenges as opportunities to do something monumental. With the highest goal in mind, they develop lives full of joy and enthusiasm no matter what obstacles they face.

You can live that way, too—in fact, you already have lived this way when you worked through a crisis that forced you to draw on your greatest resources and act naturally from the highest goal. I want you to consider bringing that same focus and flow into your everyday life. When you act from the highest goal over and over again, you slowly discover that you are traveling your own path.

This is the key to grabbing on to your highest goal: You have your own way—your own inner power, your own contribution, your own methods and approaches, and your own experience of the highest goal. Once you recognize this, your life can be a quest to discover your path and live from it. You accept that obstacles or tests contain powerful lessons and opportunities. You see that when you give yourself fully to life and the highest goal, as you do naturally when you are tested, a grace infuses you. Something helps and supports you, even though it doesn't necessarily do so in the way you might expect or in the time you might prefer.

Focusing on One Crisis

To see this grace at work in your own life, please remember a particular time when you were able to surmount a crisis or come up with something to deal with a situation or solve a problem. Please pick one situation now and contemplate it. It doesn't have to be an earth-shaking crisis or traumatic event—just something that was important to you.

As you think about this situation, ask yourself, what happened before, during and after the crisis? What did you experience, think and feel? What approaches did you use? What was surprising to you? Close your eyes and reexperience the event, if you wish.

What crisis situation did you remember? What happened? Did you get a connection to spirit or energy or grace? Did you see others in a positive way? Did your mind stop its wandering and focus? Whatever happened, remember that experience and how you actually lived through it. You might recall the way Tom Siporin lived through all the crises in his life, but now focus on your particular way and what worked for you in this situation.

Jot down some notes of what happened. Tell somebody else about it. Use any way you wish to recall, reexperience and affirm how you were able to deal with this crisis.

That memory can help you build on what works for you. As you recognize the power of that experience and the grace operating in your own life, you have made a beginning on traveling your own path.

Your Path as a Hero's Journey

Mythologists, notably Joseph Campbell, tell us that every experience of life can be seen as a hero's journey: The challenges the hero faces, the forces of good and evil, the resolution, are similar—often amazingly so—across time, place and culture.

Fairy tales, legends, myths, movies, tales of all sorts, follow this archetypal story line: Innocent (or at least naïve) hero answers a call to venture out of innocence and is initiated into situation fraught with danger. With the help of allies, hero meets challenge and returns home triumphant. Once you're familiar with the elements, you'll recognize the hero's journey that takes place in the biblical story of "Jonah and the Whale," in "Snow White" and in *The Shawshank Redemption*. Wildly different settings and details notwithstanding, each of these stories plays out the metaphorical hero's journey.

These same hero's journeys occur over and over again in your life, too. Understanding the hero's journey and recognizing it playing out in your life can help you follow your own path to the highest goal.

Characters on the hero's journey (including you!) go through six stages: Innocence, The Call, Initiation, Allies, Breakthrough, and Celebration. It's helpful to visualize these stages of the hero's journey as places on a path, as the accompanying figure illustrates. Think of these stages in terms of your own life: innocence in the womb; a call to life at birth; initiation in the difficult trials of the cold world; find-

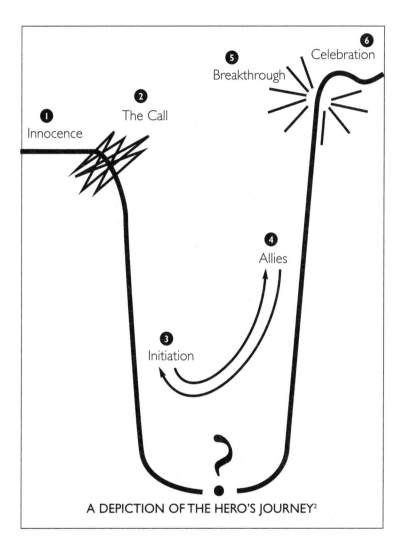

A DEPICTION OF THE HERO'S JOURNEY[2]

ing allies in your parents; breakthroughs as you learned to talk, walk and manage by yourself; and celebration as an almost immediate act with each new step.

But the hero's journey kept happening over and over again, as you left home, entered school and "were nothing." After a time, you were in the highest primary grade and celebrating. Then you entered high school and were nothing again. And so on you travel, through one hero's journey after another, learning as you go and developing your own particular style.

Every one of these stages bestows a gift: Innocence deepens the lessons from the previous journey and offers a chance for renewal. The Call energizes you and gets you moving. Initiation strengthens your skills and sharpens your sense of yourself and what you need to do. Allies give you support for the adventure. Breakthrough takes you into a new world. And Celebration generates joy and instills practices that can help you as you undertake your next journey.

Think about the hero's journey you're on right now—for you are on one, even if you don't know it. Take a moment to think about what stage you're in. Keep it in mind, and use the power of knowing to help you on your hero's journey.

Julia Romaine, a consultant, coach and Creativity in Business teacher, has learned to pay attention as she experiences hero's journeys again and again. She recognized several hero's journeys in her life as she spearheaded an initiative to bring the creativity work to the families of the victims of the World Trade Center attack.

Julia worked with 9/11 widows to formulate the idea, presented it to a foundation to get a pilot program funded, fashioned with others a "Creative Insight: Taking the First Steps" version of the course, taught the course and developed a team of instructors, sought further funding, and expanded the program. The widows in her expanding program were not only an inspiration to Julia, they were extremely grateful to her.

Then, even as Julia experienced success, she hit a wall.

A large group was going through a second round of the program, with more sessions scheduled and ample funding. Participants couldn't find words to describe the deep positive effects of the work. But Julia found it harder and harder to continue the organizing and teaching. "I don't feel passionate about this," she told a group of us. "I'm missing the first pilot group. They were the reason I was doing this. I know in my heart that I'm doing the right work, but the logistics of making it happen have taken the wind out of my sails."

As she spoke to us about it, we became her allies, and one of us reminded her of the hero's journey. Julia was, once again, at the beginning of a journey. She realized that she had to accept a new call, to work through the initiation stage of starting again. And she had allies to help her do it.

When one of us shared that he had learned how he needed to delegate certain tasks—like handling many logistical details— Julia was able to see a refinement on her path. She realized this was a test she would work through. She was resolute. She began to accept and let things play out. She didn't repress her feelings but rather moved toward them and understood them and acted on what she learned: She realized she could ask someone else to handle the logistical details.

With tears of relief in her eyes, she moved out of the initiation stage—the pit or the low point we hit before we begin, with the help of allies, to climb up toward a breakthrough. The hero's journey gave her the perspective she needed to move to the next level on her path.

Getting into a Cycle of Recognition

When you engage life from the highest goal, you are given what seem to be heroic tasks. Know that your earlier life experiences prepare you for succeeding tasks so that you can take them on with strength and ability. But you must pay attention and learn from each journey.

I've seen that people who handle crises and learn from them know that this work toward the highest goal is essential for health, happiness, success, and making a contribution in life. Know, like them, that this is a task of utmost importance.

Everyone, including you, has great power and creativity within that allows him or her to deal with the challenges life presents. You can learn how to acknowledge and act from your creativity naturally, without ego. And as you do, you'll begin to depend on it without even thinking about it.

Even though your inner resources are obscured by fear, judgment and the constant chattering of your mind (what in this book I call the VOJ, or Voice of Judgment, the inner voice of blame and criticism), you can focus on the beneficial cycle of recognizing your own connections to the highest goal.

When you travel this cycle, you are practicing one of the core discoveries I have made in my creativity work: You can consistently live from your highest goal by simply paying attention to the times when you are connected to it.

You did this earlier when you relived and concentrated on a time when you successfully dealt with a crisis. Julia did it by recognizing that she was at a stage of the hero's journey. Every time you pay attention to your own creative acts in this way you increase the probability that you'll live from your inner creativity in future situations.

It is analogous to what sports psychologists call "muscle memory." When you watch a videotape of your own or someone else's perfect performance, you increase your own ability in ways that are equivalent to hours of practice in which every move you make is perfect.

That's the beneficial cycle I'm suggesting. When you act from the highest goal and acknowledge and celebrate your break-throughs, you develop more strength for dealing with new challenges. Keep doing this and you are developing your path.

Start paying attention to the moments when you do the right thing, act appropriately, come up with an idea, or help someone who needs help. At first you will find it difficult to pay attention to your highest acts because your inner, critical Voice of Judgment will put them down. But, eventually, you'll find that the possibilities are endless. By staying conscious, you'll develop your own path and see what works for you in all kinds of situations, especially difficult ones that test you.

Over time you'll begin to see that, almost without thinking, you can strengthen yourself for a new challenge by drawing on the power of your experience dealing with a similar situation in the past. That is, your consciousness and celebration of one of your heroic acts (which is, in fact, the cumulative power of your many creative experiences recognized and celebrated) can fuel your ability to thrive and contribute in new situations.

Eventually you'll realize that your creativity, your way of bringing out your highest and acting on it, is unique. You take your own path whether you realize it or not. It's fun to discover your own way and to live from that.

If you don't do things in your way, you will be subject to pain and difficulties. If you can find what is right for you and your own style of doing it, you'll experience a life beyond imagination with contribution and fulfillment and inner peace and joy.

In our creativity course at Stanford we use a massing principle. Because creativity is idiosyncratic, we assume that any particular approach or exercise will work for only a minority of people. So we offer all kinds of approaches in the hope that something will work for each individual.

For any particular exercise, perhaps fifty percent will find that it doesn't work; thirty percent might find it unpleasant; ten per cent might even find it abhorrent; but the remaining ten percent find it useful. And among those who find it useful, five percent or even one percent may find that it creates the key to a complete life for them.

In a similar spirit, if you can stay open to all the approaches of this book and try them with openness and diligence, you are bound to find your own idiosyncratic, but ultimately effective path to the highest goal.

Staying and Thriving on Your Path

At this point you may be saying to yourself, "I've heard this before. I know that I have to have confidence in myself. I know that I can surmount obstacles sometimes. I can see that this cycle of noticing and applying my best times can be powerful. But I don't think anything is going to happen overnight."

You're right. We seldom make progress toward a fulfilled, complete, contributing life just by knowing something. A new perspective can change our lives only if it is applied consistently. It's hard for any of us to stay with any approach that promises to bring out our best or even help us deal with a specific issue.

So how can you stay with this one?

By always keeping the highest goal in mind. This, too, is a practice: When I have a conflict with someone, for instance, I stop and think of my highest goal of connecting to God and having resonance with a higher power, which is my way of thinking of the highest goal. I see that person as a teacher. I feel the love I have for them, even if they are attacking me in some way. I trust that we will both gain from the situation and accept that it has to happen. I'm not passive, because I am drawing on my inner resources and remaining open to whatever the situation has to give me and whatever comes to me in response to it. I learn from it and celebrate the grace that seems to be present.

I've found that once you have the highest goal in mind, you can deal with recurring problems or patterns in terms of the lessons they offer. For instance, because I was the youngest in my family (my only sibling, my brother Dick, was over ten years older, and I had cousins who were over twenty years older), I developed both a sense of alienation and of timidity about doing the right thing. Neither alienation nor timidity offers much in terms of moving to the highest goal as I see it.

Sure enough, tests throughout my life have pushed me away from these traits. But only since I have had the highest goal in mind have I been able to deal effectively with these recurring patterns. Although I am far from completely eliminating them, I'm able to stay the course because I see these challenges in context. And with each test I learn more about my path and stay more firmly on it.

A Beneficial Addiction

Even if you don't know exactly what the highest goal is for you, you begin a life of fulfillment just by paying attention and committing energy to your path. Once you do that, you draw grace into your life. It just happens.

I remember a young girl who was doing a daily yogic practice, which was to chant a rather long Sanskrit text. She noticed in the English translation that the chant promised that singing it daily would lead to realization of the "four goals of life (*dharma,* righteousness; *artha,* wealth; *kama,* pleasure; *moksha,* liberation)." So the girl told her mother that she was chanting in order to realize the second goal, wealth. She wanted a million dollars.

As time went on, however, she dropped her interest in the million dollars. She did the chant simply because she enjoyed it and the way it made her feel. She experienced peace and joy while she chanted the text and noticed that when she started her day with the chant, she was more centered than on other days.

Her life began to embody a movement toward the highest goal, which had turned into *moksha,* or liberation, through the grace she experienced when she did the chant.

In the same way, the more you develop and stay on your own path, the more self-worth and purpose you have, and the more you will want the rewards that support a meaningful life. Your experience of the highest goal will become its own reward, a beneficial addiction that can increase the meaning of your life and the transformation of the world.

Live with
the Highest Goal

EVERYONE HAS AT LEAST ONE recurring issue, problem or
obstacle that is pivotal in his or her life. Whether you're feeling the effects of yours right now or not, you still have something that keeps coming back in different forms. What is it for you?
What's a problem, obstacle or issue that you face that if it could be
solved, overcome or dealt with, would lead to an *immeasurable*
change for the better in your life?

Please take a moment to think about this. Focus on something pivotal in your life, an issue that comes up repeatedly, albeit in
different forms. It may or may not be affecting you now in terms of
a specific issue, but you know that it will surface again sooner or
later. Don't pick a problem as specific as finding a new job or as cosmic as determining the purpose of your existence; focus on a "middle range" issue, something between those extremes.

Depending on their personalities and current circumstances,
people's recurring issue may bother them a lot or a little. But often

they don't see the underlying pattern or how it repeats endlessly in their lives. And they don't realize that resolving it can lead them to the highest goal and to fulfilling dreams they didn't know they had.

Often this issue has something to do with the fundamental objective of finding purpose and meaning in life. In decades of teaching creativity at Stanford and elsewhere and asking this question of thousands of people, I've learned that these problems of the middle range come from five major life challenges: finding prosperity, dealing with time and stress, developing relationships that work, achieving balance, and bringing your creativity into the world. We'll delve into those challenges in the next five chapters of this book.

What's Your Problem?

What's the most pressing issue for you? Don't pick one for someone else's approval. Don't strive for something big from an external perspective. Just think about a problem that comes to mind almost immediately, even if life in general is going well for you now. Think about how that current issue or obstacle represents a problem of the middle range, something recurring and fundamental for you.

When you've got something, jot down what's important about its nature, what causes its persistence, how it affects your life, what you've tried so far to deal with it, and how life might be if you didn't have that problem. At the same time, notice if its underlying nature is similar to one of the five challenges—prosperity, time and stress, relationships, balance, and sharing your creativity.

Now keep that problem—both the current urgent aspect and the recurring underlying aspect—in mind as you go through the journey of this book. See when, as a result of being on this journey, you get some resolution on the problem. Or when you finish this chapter you might want to jump ahead to one of the final five chapters to explore approaches to the particular challenge you have.

The Error of Ignoring Oneness and Connection

Through the journey of this book, you will begin to see your problem and others in a larger context. You will see that the biggest problem you have is that you do not live your life from a trust in the oneness and connection in life; you do not live completely from the highest goal.

Systems theorists tell us that we make a big mistake when we try to solve individual problems. Everything—including us—is linked to everything else in the world and all its individual parts. If we solve one problem, we are likely to get kicked in the pants by another. Or the original problem in an unfamiliar guise returns to trip us up yet again.

Take the relatively straightforward example of our body's system. When we solve the problem of a headache by taking an analgesic or ibuprofen, for instance, it may cause us to become drowsy and lose motor control—thus, we create another problem. And the headache's underlying cause, which might be serious and systemic, still lives in our body because we haven't dealt with its role in the whole system.

Consider the experience of a participant in the creativity course, who was moving into a new kind of work that was more fulfilling for him. His first problem was that he couldn't figure out how to market his offering; once he did, however, he found that he had created another problem:

My fear may not have been fear of failure, but fear of success. I can't tell you the momentary panic I felt when I got . . . the phone call with "This is perfect—we've been looking for a program EXACTLY like this for our people." YIKES!!! You know what that means? It means I have to come up with "the goods." Scary as hell.

He was able to channel that fear by seeing his new problem in a larger context and remembering the highest goal. Even with that perspective, however, most of us need more help to keep us going on the path to transformation.

Yes, information is essential. It is important to know, as the systems theorists tell us and sages have been urging in different ways over the millennia, that there is oneness and connection with everything. But look at any system—even one as small as the human body—and you see complexity beyond the mind's ability to comprehend. How can we cope with all the systems in our lives without really understanding them in detail?

Heuristics as a Way of Life

The answer I have discovered—the centerpiece of the effectiveness of the creativity work—is to start living from heuristics. Heuristics are generalizations or rules of thumb for insight and learning. You can think of them as admonitions, mottoes for living or, as I call them in this book, live-withs. They are open directions for living that thousands of people have used along their path to transformation.

Every one of this book's chapter titles—for example, "Go Beyond Passion and Success," "Travel Your Own Path," "Live with the Highest Goal"—is a live-with. And in addition, each of the later chapters of the book suggests a live-with—such as See with Your Heart, or Yes or No?—that you can use to bring the ideas of that chapter into your life. (Appendix B, at the end of the book, lists live-withs we have used in the course throughout the years for various purposes.)

Live-withs are not affirmations. They are not prescriptions that tell you exactly what to do. Rather, they call you to new ways of behaving that bring out your best. Most important, they urge you to draw on your inner resources and create your path in relation to the relevant systems in your life. In short, they lead to your living with the highest goal. The truth is that the best way to achieve the highest goal is to start living with it. And live-withs are the best way to do this, bit by bit.

Want to generate more faith in your inner resources and your journey with the highest goal? Try living for a week with the live-with, Have No Expectations. Take the risk of preparing, having a clear intention and then relying on your resources without attachment to the way things are supposed to turn out. You'll develop an almost visceral understanding—your own understanding—of the difference between expectations and goals or intentions. You'll experience openness. As you consciously observe what happens when you try the Have No Expectations live-with in your own way, you begin to build up faith in your inner resources and learn what works for you in your quest for the highest goal.

Similarly, if you want to eliminate the weakening influence of the inner chattering of blame and criticism, the Voice of Judgment, or VOJ, try living with the heuristic Psych Out the VOJ. Since the VOJ consists of voices of other people, primarily your parents, it isn't really your essential Self. When you live with Psych Out the VOJ, you become your essential Self and trick this dysfunctional marauder. Try the live-with for a while, and you'll start to distance yourself from the VOJ, live more often from your Essence and connect with the highest goal more frequently.

To develop your capacity for being conscious and present, try Pay Attention. This live-with moves you into precise observation, where you can see with the objectivity of a scientist and the wonder of a child. People living with Pay Attention often observe something—like a child playing, a sunset, a piece of music, the movement of water—that connects them to the highest goal.

To move to a new level of asking penetrating questions, live with Ask Dumb Questions for a week or so. The word "dumb" can allow you to get beyond the fears and nattering of the VOJ that tells you not to ask questions when they actually should be asked. People find that when they take the leap and ask a sincere question of clarity, others thank them for opening things up and getting to the heart of the matter.

By bringing live-withs into your life, especially when they are connected to particular practices (as are the live-withs above) or challenges (as are the live-withs in the following chapters), you let the systems of your life speak to you. When you engage life with Have No Expectations, for instance, you begin to see all the ways *your* expectations affect *you* in the systems of *your* life. You stay open without expectation and experience *your* inner resources and *your* connection to *your* highest goal.

Notice that live-withs often challenge misconceptions you might have. Often they might surprise you. You might think, for instance, "Have no expectations? If I didn't have expectations, I wouldn't have anything to motivate me." You can argue endlessly about such issues. But when you live with Have No Expectations, try new approaches and are conscious about what happens, you learn for yourself the damaging effects of specific expectations, the motivation of intention and the power of having a positive attitude that is connected to the highest goal.

Your first reaction to a live-with may be that it is impossible, absurd or stupid. But work with it anyway, notice your reactions, reserve judgment, and ask penetrating questions about your reactions: Why do I find this live-with so hard? What is behind my reactions? What am I afraid to let go? How can I overcome my blocks to this?

You will often have breakthroughs just by considering each live-with. One woman was living with Have No Expectations when she attended a professional conference. Realizing she often had expectations of such an industry event, she kept reminding herself to let go of them. She developed a way to let go of each expectation: recognizing it, feeling amused at her overactive mind and then letting it go. "This was very freeing," she said. "I felt more relaxed and in the flow. I was able to go with whatever was happening and whatever I was feeling. I loved it! It is a challenging [live-with] to maintain, and one that I want to continue."

When you apply a live-with to your life, you have to apply it to whatever is in front of you. You might be facing a continuing problem with meetings. You might be worrying about making an assertion you need to make to a boss or a loved one. You might be getting and giving less than you think is possible in weekend times with your family. You might be stumped in dealing with what seems like a life-or-death issue at work.

Try a live-with in the context of these situations, and see what happens. Sometimes there is a big shift. One director of a software company found that when she led meetings without expectations, they opened up and became lively and productive. People who never spoke became major contributors.

Even minor shifts can make meaningful changes in your life. One man was dissatisfied with Saturdays. Everyone in his family tried to cram all the errands that didn't get done during the week into Saturdays, and so the day was filled with tension and distance. But when he lived with Have No Expectations, the day opened up for the whole family. They tried an activity they hadn't done before and got into flow with it. He saw the value of breaking patterns in all parts of his life.

Sometimes the shift is more subtle but profound. A woman who was living with Have No Expectations was conflicted about whether to apply for the job of her boss who had just left. She began to notice all the negative assertions or expectations that were stopping her. Then she was able to watch those and distance herself from them. She knew that she would apply for the position, but the experience that led to this realization, which was an experience of the highest goal, was more important to her. "Suddenly I have a sense that there is a lot of space around me," she said. "Things don't feel so tight and limited [living] with no expectations. I'm smiling a lot now."

Getting the Most Out of Live-Withs

There is an aphorism, "Knowledge is bondage." Isn't it true? Doesn't what we know often get in the way of our essential wisdom? Don't we often know something, but not put it into practice in our lives? If we put knowledge into practice and pay attention to what happens, we can develop our own approaches for living that move us closer to the highest goal.

Consider what has happened over the years in the creativity course at Stanford. We rarely talk directly about the highest goal. Yet people leave the course with a determination and a path to live with the highest goal. And alums carry this forward in the way they live their lives. Why? Live-withs. They're the primary reason the course moves people to the highest goal.

You can have this benefit also. You can conquer your challenges, find your path and live with the highest goal, without even thinking about it. But live-withs can work this way only if you do them consciously as part of a discipline that keeps you focused on what is right for you.

When you practice a live-with, try it for a week. You can do them for a longer or shorter time, but you'll get more benefit if you take enough time to try them out. After you have some experiences with a live-with, write a page or so reflecting on what happened.

You can decide whether you want to do this, but we've learned that writing about your experiences increases the opportunity that you'll learn from them. Even telling someone else about them helps. Whether you write or talk or both, you will benefit from feedback. This feedback is essential, no matter what its form, because it helps you celebrate your experience, correct course and get ready for the next live-with.

It's this cycle—of acknowledging and learning about your challenge, consciously living with a live-with that relates to it, reflecting and writing about your experience, and sharing with someone else who can give you feedback—that will move you toward living with the highest goal.

Take, for instance, Go Beyond Passion and Success, the live-with that is the title of Chapter 1. If you read just that chapter and practice the implied live-with in your life in your own way, reflect on your experience and get feedback from someone else, you will begin a new approach to life—from the perspective of the highest goal rather than the sub-optimizing that is suggested by our culture.

The live-withs Find True Prosperity, Turn Fears into Breakthroughs, Relate from Your Heart, Experience Synergy in Every Moment, and Become a Generative Leader, which are also the titles of Chapters 4 through 8, suggest ways to begin to understand and grow from the challenges examined therein. Further, each of those chapters contains a live-with that you can use to take action on the discoveries in the chapter and move yourself to a higher place of understanding and skill.

We have a tendency in this culture to expect results on even the biggest challenge immediately or, if not then, shortly thereafter. We look for a magic pill that will cure all of our ills. But moving toward the highest goal is a long-term process—filled with tests and glorious moments, to be sure, but still a long haul. So don't worry whether you are doing a live-with "correctly." Just experiment and see what works for you. This is a way of life in which little things count. Take every opportunity to notice your blessings when they occur. As they say, "Little steps make big feats."

Whether it's a live-with, a new approach to a problem, or just a notable experience, work at making it your own. For the live-with Pay Attention, for instance, some people go to a spot in nature and pay attention to everything they see. Others make a list of all the things they should be paying attention to (but normally don't) and work through that list. Some concentrate on listening. Others find it helpful to try specific exercises we suggest in the course.

People take an amazing variety of approaches to exploring and learning from each live-with. More important than your approach, however, is the resolution with which you continue the process. You must have faith and stay with what works. When you try something new, it may not seem successful, but challenge yourself and try to experience your approach consistently. You will make steps forward whether you realize it in the moment or not.

This process is experiential, not intellectual. When you do these live-withs, you are in an experiential mode that can move you further than you thought possible. Which is not to say you lose your intellectual capabilities; on the contrary, you strengthen them by giving them more to work with. You simply quit allowing them to prevent you from experiencing life.

The deeper you go in experiencing each live-with, the more you will get out of it. At a minimum you can reflect on what you did, what the experience was like, how it felt and what the results were. But you can go deeper by getting into a flow, experimenting with something different and incorporating it into your life moment by moment so it eventually becomes more natural. And then you can go even deeper by contemplating what you've experienced, looking for insights, determining how to apply the lessons of the live-with to your challenges, and looking for implications for your journey to the highest goal.

Labeling experiences as good or bad can get in the way of getting value out of the live-with. Even when you can't break that pattern, however, you can get something—often a lot—out of a live-with if you keep reflecting on it. If you take the time to write your reflection, you'll get even more. At least ten percent of the weekly papers I get from Stanford students start out with something like: "This was a terrible week to live with Do Only What You Love, Love Everything You Do. I didn't have a good experience at all." As students continue to reflect, however, they often write something so moving it brings tears to my eyes. In the end, even they conclude, "Well, I guess I did get something out of that after all."

As you do live-withs and experience them in your life, skip the labeling stage and go directly to simply observing what is happening to you, moment by moment. Know that there are no good or bad experiences, only experiences you learn from and those you don't learn from because you are busy labeling them.

The experience of a woman who was offering the creativity work to women lawyers serves to illustrate. She was a legal specialist, but this course was new territory. The week she was starting the program, she was living with Live Your Passion. At the same time, she was moving to a new home and hosting out-of-town visitors. Even as she sat in what she described as "the midst of boxes, books, dust, general upheaval and angst," she was able to observe what she was actually experiencing. "If you could see the faces of the women about to embark upon this journey, your spirits would soar," she exulted. "I am convinced that when we move from this place of passion, it gives hope to others that they may also live from a place that feeds their spirit and nourishes the soul."

When she shared her reflection with others, she got feedback about how she had changed in important ways. "I hear something new in your voice in this reflection . . . something I haven't heard before, though it must have been there all along," one of her colleagues wrote. "It's hard to describe, but it is about loving, moving and growing rather than fighting, defending and overcoming. It seems that your warrior self has moved into a new stage and it sounds very powerful, as if you're using your energy in a profoundly different way. It's beautiful and inspiring to see."

Of course, this woman isn't finished with her journey, but she now celebrates a stronger sense of herself. And she can see how this connection to the highest goal can help her on her adventures to come.

An Ancient Trick You Can Use: Bootstrapping

People all over the world chant certain words and melodies and get benefits ranging from feelings of peace or energy, to creative inspiration, to well-being and joy. From Gregorian chants in the West to mantras in the East, these sounds can awaken the highest in those who sing or say them and in those who just listen to them.

I wondered why these particular syllables and tones could have these effects. Then I discovered that they came from ancient sages and seekers who achieved connections to the highest goal. They experienced states of equanimity, peace, bliss, and truth that they had been seeking. And they also heard celestial music and words, the sounds of voices in song.

After a time they began to remember the specific things they heard, and then they tried to reverse the process. In other words, they started making the sounds that they heard when they were in a high state so they could get back into that high state. These sounds became the mantras and the basis of chants that people use to get into high states even today.

I suggest that you do this process too, which is a little like bootstrapping. But instead of reproducing music, re-create in a new situation the inner experience you had when you have operated at a high level, been creative or dealt with a crisis in an effective way.

Use this approach as you try live-withs and as you are conscious about your own creative experiences. Use it especially when you have strong positive experiences in dealing with crises or in situations that bring you joy. When you are in a new situation that requires that you bring out your best, recall the experience you had in an earlier successful situation, and bring it into the new one. You can do this in terms of remembering your experience in a feeling sense. Or you can do this by reminding yourself that you were able to handle a difficult situation in the past, even when you thought there was no hope.

Essentially I'm suggesting that as you live your life as a live-with process, notice the heuristics that work for you, live with them and then strengthen your own best behavior by expanding upon your past breakthroughs in new situations. Try this way of living starting right now, and use the rest of this book to help you with this process.

The Secret in Action:
Decades of Living with the Highest Goal

Don Maruska participated in the first offering of the personal creativity course at Stanford. He went on to become the award-winning
CEO of three Silicon Valley companies. When he visited the class as
a guest speaker, he impressed the students with how he had imbibed
its lessons and fashioned them into his own life. He spoke of the
highest goal in terms of some Eastern approaches we used in the
course and of the sustenance he received from the church he
attended.

Then Don and his wife, Liz, a noted artist, made a major
change in their lives, partially for health reasons but also because
they were looking for new directions. They moved out of the San
Francisco Bay Area and about two hundred miles south to the sea-
side town of Morro Bay. Don severed formal ties with his companies
in the north, and he and his family began a new life.

Certain aspects of the move were difficult for Don because
he missed the familiarity and excitement of life in Silicon Valley. But
he persevered in a new direction, bolstered by an approach to decision making and team building that he developed with an Episcopal
priest. His love for his wife and daughter kept him seeing what was
possible.

Eventually, he became one of the top business coaches in the
country. He uses his decision-making approach to help groups of
people turn conflict into new directions and collaboration. He also
writes a column called "Business Success" that is distributed by the
Knight-Ridder syndicate to over two hundred newspapers. In it he
sometimes tells his readers about live-withs.

In his columns and in a book (*How Great Decisions Get Made*) that he has written about his decision-making approach, he invokes his highest goal, which is based on the experience of oneness and flow he achieves in working with groups. He sees himself as a bridge that links together people, ideas and opportunities to bring out the best in everyone. And that calling is based on "the great commandment to love and glorify God and to love one another as thyself."

I once asked Don to write about his over twenty-five years of living with the creativity work. He said that the process has encouraged him to "found three Silicon Valley companies, recover from adversities, become an author and business coach, and enjoy a creative and fulfilling life."

Of course, Don is still on his journey and faces new challenges regularly. He brings substantial resources to that task, some of which you are about to draw on as we move to your major life challenges. Carry with you the issue, your problem of the middle range, that you chose at the beginning of this chapter. See what happens as you enter into the powerful live-with process.

Find True Prosperity

WITHOUT A DOUBT, at one point or another in your life, you've experienced that "Is that all there is?" feeling. You get something you want—a car, a home, a special relationship, a promotion, a windfall of money, a degree, an award— yet your feeling of achievement soon fades to dissatisfaction. So you pick yourself up and start working harder than ever to reach the next plateau. Once you reach it, you experience the same discontent, look to the next goal, and jump into the whole cycle again. And so it goes.

This is the heart of the challenge to find true prosperity: In our culture, we look for prosperity outside ourselves, and all the while it waits for us internally.

True prosperity is being happy and continuously experiencing the variety and infinity of qualities that make up your Self. That is the way you can touch the experience of the highest goal. You achieve true prosperity by having a full, rich feeling of self-worth.

Finding true prosperity in the midst of a culture that urges you to deny the power of the highest goal requires awareness and action. You first must recognize that you are like a fish caught in a powerful ocean current that pushes you to ignore and even depreciate your inner resources. Once you become aware, you can begin building faith in your inner resources and become conscious of your own self-worth. You do this by experimenting with discovering and doing the things you love and dropping those you hate. The more you concentrate on recognizing your highest qualities, expressing them and having faith in them, the more you will experience the self-worth that is true prosperity.

In a sense, the search for true prosperity encapsulates the advantages of focusing on the highest goal. If you aim for the highest goal, over time you'll discover your purpose and prosperity. You'll live with a sense of prosperity—with or without the external rewards that our culture touts as happiness. Material bounty may well be the by-product of your spiritual bounty, but it won't be your focus.

You'll be better able to cope with the eventuality of change and loss of money, possessions, employment, relationships, appearance, and health. The highest goal will help you face these challenges with the strength to learn from them.

What's Your Challenge?

We are all pulled away from true prosperity. Do you find yourself worrying about money or other external rewards? Do you find yourself on a roller coaster of elation or sadness, depending on how things are going at the moment? Do you find yourself envying others who seem to have it all together? Do you have a low opinion of yourself? What is the nature of your prosperity challenge? What long-term prosperity problem, issue or obstacle would you like to solve, handle or remove using the direction of this chapter?

Through teaching the creativity course at Stanford University, I've discovered that for most people, their relationship to money and prosperity goes back to incidents in their childhood. When students examine events that contribute to these deep feelings and recognize their impact, they can choose to live differently, especially if they have the broad perspective of true prosperity.

For example, one student told the class about the day her mother died. Her father brought in a bowl of strawberries. Her mother loved strawberries, but just as she was about to eat them, she said, "Strawberries are out of season. They must be so expensive now. Why did you spend all that money for them?" And those were her last words.

Her daughter's work on this moment in our class moved her to a new understanding of her challenge with money and search for true prosperity. As she vowed never to be that stingy and obsessed with money, she began to make the shift from a scarcity mentality to an abundance mentality.

Consider now the nature of your prosperity challenge. See if you can put your true prosperity challenge into a sentence or two. Or try drawing it. Or, since most stories have something to do with people trying to find happiness, consider a movie or story that represents your challenge with finding and living with true prosperity. When you understand something about what the prosperity challenge is for you, take a moment to consider the work you have to do to turn this challenge into an opportunity.

Money Versus Faith

It requires enormous faith, abiding faith, to live from the highest goal and find true prosperity in self-worth.

But what is this faith? In the most well known Christian definition, Saint Paul says in his letter to the Hebrews, "Now faith is the substance of things hoped for, the evidence of things not seen."

Then Paul tells stories of faith; he describes Abraham going forth, even though he didn't know at first where he was going. These stories provide a model for your journey within and toward the highest goal. Because the highest goal is embedded in everything, all encompassing and yet individual to you at the same time, you must embark on your journey without lesser goals and proceed with faith, learning as you go. Only this kind of faith can make the journey possible; otherwise, you end up taking someone else's journey or a journey that doesn't bring the highest goal into your life.

Consider the enormity of Paul's definition. What could possibly be the substance of things hoped for? How can you have evidence of things not seen? Perhaps you've already answered those questions as you thought about situations in which you have resonance with the highest goal. The substance and the evidence of faith live within you, not outside.

The late American art historian, educator and artist Mary Holmes adds similar insight when she says, "Faith is the only way that we can accept the fact that we don't know the future, but are still able to imagine it and act on it." Without this kind of faith, it is as if we are paralyzed. The writer and poet George Franklin agrees when he says that to deny one's own inner life and resources through a lack of faith "is to be cruelly impoverished."

Your Moments of Truth

Of course when you try to live with this abiding faith, you come up against a Catch-22. That is, you know about and develop faith in your inner resources and their connection to the highest goal by having experiences of them. But you have to have faith in the first place to do what leads to those experiences.

There is a story told about a spiritual teacher and his student who came to the edge of a cliff. There was a seven-foot gap over a deep crevice that separated them from solid land on the other side. Suddenly the teacher said to the student, "Jump." Without thinking, the student jumped and alighted easily on the other side. The story tells us that the teacher knew that the student was ready and had faith in him. And the student had developed adequate faith in the teacher and in himself so that he could accept a seemingly inappropriate command and experience his own greatness.

Lawyer and international expert in conflict resolution Julian Gresser shared a similar story with one of my classes. As part of his own personal development, he worked with a widely recognized hatha yoga master. Julian had accomplished many difficult hatha yoga poses, but he was not able to do one seemingly impossible pose in which the body would be held off the ground horizontally with just hands and forearms. He had seen his yoga teacher do it, but no matter how hard he tried, he couldn't do it.

Then one day they were walking down a forest path and the master told Julian to do the pose right there, right then. Just like the student in the story, Julian acted immediately. He got on the ground, placed his hands and did the pose for the first time. It seemed to happen with no effort. And after that he could do it over and over with relative ease.

After he told this story to the Stanford class, he demonstrated the pose. The students gathered around in a circle. Julian took off the jacket of his three-piece suit, and, miraculously, he seemed to float about a foot off the floor, held up by just his forearms.

These stories give us direction for dealing with the paradox of faith: We must have enough faith to do the acts that give us an experience of faith. As with all paradoxes, we need to see the bigger picture in order to deal with it. By seeing the hatha yoga position as part of a larger practice of developing himself and doing better work in the world, Julian Gresser was able to do the miraculous pose with ease. Everything, including finding faith in your path toward true prosperity, happens in the form of a hero's journey and presents you with challenges. You may toil for a long time in different ways before you reach a breakthrough.

An ancient Indian scripture, the Shiva Sutras, sums up this resolution to the paradox of faith in its seventeenth sutra, or teaching: "Knowledge of the Self is firm conviction." That is, you can reach a point, if you work at it, in which your faith and your highest goal are the same.

Live-With:
Do Only What You Love, Love Everything You Do

Now it is time to live as if you have true prosperity, whatever the nature of your challenge. Try living with the admonition "Do Only What You Love, Love Everything You Do" for at least a week. Notice what you experience. Live as much as possible as if you are in true prosperity, doing the things that you love to do and experiencing the things you have to do in a way that allows you to love that time, too.

Know that when you live this way, you are living in resonance with the highest goal. Some traditions consider doing dharma (your role in life, right livelihood) on a regular basis to be achieving the highest goal. Others put it in terms of being in flow or being in the Tao, the natural order of life. When you live with this live-with, you will have moments in which you experience these connections to the highest goal.

See what living this way tells you about both your Self and Work. Notice whether, when you really pay attention, you really love those activities you think you love. Track the effort you have to exert to do things you love to do. See what the benefits are, as well as the difficulties, when you take time to do what you love.

Do this live-with no matter what your week is like, no matter what your pressures. Some people find that stopping to take time to do something they love gives them renewed energy for the work they have to do. Time changes for them. They get into flow. They sense space opening for them to live from the highest.

Prosperity is a lot about space, about having the time to be yourself and do the things that nurture your Self, as psychologist and human resources professional Pamela Mayer puts it.[1] Every time you do something you love, you experience the space of renewal. You see that the source of the love that you feel is a connection between yourself and the highest goal.

Just as with any live-with, you can practice this on four levels of increasing depth:

1. Do only what you love.
2. Love everything you do.
3. Be conscious of your experiences.
4. Get into the flow of faith, purpose and prosperity.

1. Do only what you love.

You don't need to *do* anything in particular. Just *be* fully in the world, holding your vision and allowing your purpose in life to come into focus. Throughout the week, or whatever time period you do this live-with, increase the amount of time (coming as close to one hundred percent as possible) spent only in activities that meet at least one of the following criteria:

- the activity is easy, effortless and enjoyable;
- the activity is intrinsically meaningful to you;
- the activity feels natural to do;
- the activity makes time go by quickly;
- the activity is something to look forward to;
- the activity makes you feel good about yourself;
- there is nothing you would rather be doing;
- you enjoy the activity for itself, not simply as a means to an end;
- you have the sense that you are contributing to the fulfillment of your purpose in life.

Become more aware of what you love to do, and move toward making your life a series of moments spent doing those things. Select three activities that you love to do but haven't done for quite a while. Commit to yourself, or, better yet, to someone else, that you will do all three as part of this live-with. See what happens and write down your experiences.

Although this is the first level of the live-with, it may not be easy for you because we have been trained not to do things we love as a regular practice. For instance, the head of a strategic marketing and communication company in Chicago admitted that this was very difficult for him until he discovered that his own face was telling him what he loved to do. He just had to pay attention:

> *Occasionally, for the oddest reason and at the oddest time, my mouth would break into a smile—nothing huge mind you, just a little . . . "release" around the corners of my mouth when I would be resting or looking out the window thinking about what I love to do—not actually doing it, just thinking about the possibility of what it might be—and I would find my mouth, like the Grinch, involuntarily smiling.*

The things he first thought he would do effortlessly and love to do, all turned out to be prodigious amounts of work. Instead, he discovered he loved "pretty ordinary stuff, like sitting and looking out the window or people watching, and breathing and humming and listening."

2. Love everything you do.

See difficult activities that you have to do in a larger context of your goals. A student might see a particularly rough course as a step he needs to take to graduate and do the things he wants to do. A corporate executive might see the extended road trip she has to take as part of the job of rallying her troops around an initiative.

Try changing your attitude about these things by making them fit the qualities of who you are at core. Certain techniques can be helpful: Perhaps you can play soothing music to bring out the quality of peace, work in nature for a sense of communion or work with others to bring in energy. You might make a game of activities you dislike: Try doing the most difficult, depressing and distasteful task first, then the next-most hated task, and so on, making each succeeding task a reward for the one that preceded it. Discover what works for you.

The director of a network of business, training, consulting, and creative specialists in Philadelphia found small approaches that made a difference for him. He made difficult phone calls, reached out to more prospects, vacuumed more rugs, even "de-piled" his office by using a number of stratagems. "Sometimes it was visualizing the end result; sometimes it was doing the work in tiny, bite-size chunks and between other things that made it seem effortless," he says. "Sometimes it was doing it first thing in the morning that got it over with that made the difference."

3. Be conscious of your experiences.

You'll get more out of any live-with if you are conscious of what happens when you do it. Write it down and celebrate it. Talking to others about what you have learned and getting feedback is always wise, but especially with this live-with: The value of your life is at stake.

You can learn whether the things you thought you loved to do are really as satisfying as you thought. Conversely, you can see that tasks you normally avoid are not really that bad; in fact, they can be fulfilling and lead to flow if you are consciously aware when you do them. Always ask yourself what you are getting from each activity during your practice of this live-with to add to or confirm the qualities that are part of your Essence.

A Canadian mergers and acquisitions specialist practiced this live-with when she faced an onerous task: She was doing research that required her to peruse thousands of pages of information in hundreds of boxes of documents. She struggled to find something to love about old books, dust, dim lighting, and instant headaches.

"To my surprise," she says, "I did find plenty—although it took some effort at the beginning of this task. What I found was some amazing stuff: hand-written public offerings from the late 1890s, beautiful handwriting in ledgers, precise and careful keeping of records, and so on."

She found that being conscious about an experience that seemed difficult at first had really turned it around for her. "I looked for the stories in the boxes and the pages," she says, "and came away with a clearer perspective of what I had read and what I had researched." She was excited that what she had found complemented her mission to bring myth into organizations as a healing force.

4. Get into the flow of faith, purpose and prosperity.

When you experience flow and act on your inner resources, naturally, without thinking, you have achieved the highest level of this live-with. If this happens even once during your practice, don't forget it. You can bring the sense of this experience into other situations. That will help you break the illusion that you are small and inadequate. As you build from one flow situation to another, you will feel your purpose grow in clarity and strength.

An employee development specialist in a multi-billion-dollar California company connected with her highest goal of service with love when she focused on what she loved to do. As she describes it:

> *I love to touch people in real and meaningful ways. I was never more alive, more fulfilled, more intensely aware than when I was working with dying and grieving clients at a hospice, or when I was walking with my dad through his last year of life. My purpose is to bring life (that they may have it to the full, as the Good Book says).*
>
> *And it works at all levels, in hundreds of different ways. I clean the kitchen, and serve dinner. I spent my vacation working at our church's summer camp, serving as both a member of the drama team and a team leader. I wrote an essay that touched someone's heart. I made a phone call to a friend when we were both grieving the loss of a parent. I drove a dying woman to the beach so she could see the ocean one more time. It's not just what I love to do, it's what I live to do. . . .*
>
> *I think the secret is the more I pay attention to exactly what I am doing, the easier it is to love doing it. Even cleaning toilets . . . I love having them clean, and it's an act of service (i.e., love) for family and visitors who will be using them."*

Discovering Your True Prosperity

Whether or not you do this live-with, you can learn more about what makes true prosperity for you just by paying attention to critical incidents in your life that connect you to the highest goal.

Despite the VOJ, your true nature comes out when you feel strong emotion—when you love or hate what you are doing. By looking at these critical incidents in your life, you can learn which of your inner qualities resonate with those activities you love and are missing from those you hate. And with that information, you can acknowledge and bring those qualities into everything you do, thereby achieving true prosperity.

In a sense I am suggesting that you expand the process that you did in the Most Meaningful Thing exercise in the Introduction. But now you will look at many critical incidents, many meaningful activities, many moments of joy and love, and many qualities that represent who you are at core.

So now, or when you can set aside an hour or so to discover your own prosperity, try the following exercise. (At a minimum, read it now so that you are attuned to the ways in which your highest goal appears when you do what you love.)

1. In a column on the left side of a blank page, make a list of at least twenty activities that you love to do, activities that meet at least one of the criteria that were mentioned in the live-with description. Have fun with this—keep adding to your list and enjoy thinking about these activities you love. As you make this list, leave enough space on the right side to write as many as four words.

2. In a left-side column of a new blank page, list activities you hate to do. (These are activities that meet the *reverse* of at least one of the criteria for the live-with: They are without intrinsic meaning, feel uncomfortable and unnatural to do, make time drag, and so on.) Try to get at least twenty and plow through the task, even if it is difficult. Think of it as an opportunity to vent. Remember, again, to leave space on the right side to write as many as four words.

3. Using the Qualities list shown here, write next to each love-to-do activity the quality or qualities you get from doing that activity.

4. Again, using the Qualities list, write next to each hate-to-do activity the quality or qualities that are *absent* from that activity.

5. Count the number of times each quality occurs on your lists. Tabulate this across the two lists. You will find that the same quality that makes you love activities is also missing from the activities you hate. You'll also undoubtedly find some qualities that come up relatively often, but just on one of the lists.

6. Notice not only the number of times each quality occurs, but also how they might group together: For example, Energy, Creativity, Enthusiasm, Vitality might form one grouping; likewise, Calm, Wholeness, Simplicity might combine to form another. You may find a number of these groupings for yourself. Begin to get at the richness of who you are.

QUALITIES*

Admiration	Appreciation	Beauty	Bliss	Brotherhood
Calm	Communication	Communion	Compassion	Connection
Courage	Creativity	Detachment	Energy	Enthusiasm
Entrepreneurial	Eternity	Excellence	Faith	Freedom
Friendship	Generosity	Goodness	Goodwill	Gratitude
Harmony	Humanitarian	Humor	Inclusiveness	Infinity
Joy	Liberation	Light	Love	Order
Patience	Positiveness	Power	Reality	Renewal
Quiet	Serenity	Service	Silence	Simplicity
Synthesis	Tranquility	Trust	Truth	Understanding
Vitality	Wholeness	Will	Wisdom	Wonder

*Definition: A quality is the superior characteristic or property of something. As used within this context, a life quality represents a deep attribute that characterizes an important part of one's life. It is a distinguishing property of life. A quality will correspond to something intangible that is of great value in life. It will distinguish the whole of something.

7. Look at this work as if someone else did it. What is this person like at core? Begin to own up to the fact that you have these qualities as part of your Essence. If you have time you might want to write a little vignette about who you are at core, or draw something that represents this person who is you. This vignette or drawing can go beyond the quantitative aspect of the qualities and form a new Gestalt of true prosperity for you.

If you can discover the qualities of your Essence in this way, you then know the qualities you must have in your life work to move toward the highest goal. You also will have learned the qualities that you offer in anything you do—any job, any relationship and any service you perform. Not only does this build your faith in your own inner resources, but it also gives you a way to stay on purpose and meaning in every part of your life.

Entrepreneur and venture capitalist Paul Hwoschinsky first suggested this approach to me in my class at Stanford. His seminal book, *True Wealth,* elaborated: "The connections between who we are and what we do are the conduits through which True Wealth flows."[2] In other words, the more you bring these qualities into your life, the richer you become in a larger sense.

What's more, it doesn't matter what activities you are doing; the qualities you get and give are what make a difference. We all know, if we consider the matter even a little bit, what we love to do. We may love to walk on the beach and watch a sunset, to fish, to play a particular sport, to dance with friends, read engrossing novels, or get up early in the morning and gaze at the sunrise while sipping coffee.

But, you might say, knowing these things doesn't help much because you can't make a living by walking on a beach. And what service are you providing to the world by reading an engrossing novel or playing a game? How are you helping by doing these things?

Perhaps you can answer these questions for yourself now. Now you know you don't have to do these specific activities to make a living, to serve or to help. You simply have and bring the qualities you get from these activities into what you do to make a living, to serve and to help. If you know your qualities, you can stay right where you are and use them to make your work fulfilling. With this knowledge and this approach, you can do what you love, *and* you can transform the things you have to do into activities you love.

How do people put these discoveries to work in their lives?

A systems analyst who now brings spiritual concepts into everyday life using the web and teaching, found that discovery, freedom and wonder were the qualities she needed to be truly prosperous. Once she understood this, she was able to bring them into every part of her life. "I have finally been able to put into words what I feel when I have experiences that I love," she says. "And by taking these qualities into the things I have to do, which I love a great deal less, I have literally discovered a way to live with discovery, freedom, and wonder."

Even simple experiences became richer for her. For instance, she always loved the feeling of wind on her face, though she could never explain why. After doing the love/hate lists exercise, she realized it has the qualities of Freedom, Renewal and Beauty. "For me, it is exhilarating and relaxing at the same time," she says. "But most important, it is the sense of Freedom I feel when I have the wind in my face."

At work, her heightened sense of discovery magnified her enjoyment: "I have never been so present during a normal day of work. As I maintained this sense of wonder, I felt I was in the zone. With a conscious attempt to love what I do, I found myself much more invested in my conversations with others. I was a better listener and a more passionate counselor/advisor. My conversations came more from my Essence than my Intellect."

The Secret in Action: An Inflection Point

You can live with that same grace, perhaps as a result of this live-with and the exercise in this chapter. You won't experience it in the way the people I have described here experienced it, but in a way that is exactly right for you—a way that continually expands your prosperity and your connection to the highest goal.

This is the secret of the highest goal in action. When you journey toward it and with it, your natural prosperity supports you not only in getting through the difficult times with grace but also in moving to a more enriching phase of your life. When this happens, I call it an "inflection point."

The systems analyst mentioned above, for instance, faced the task of picking up her life after her husband of twenty-one years passed away. She did this with grace and support and fashioned a new life for herself that she continually expands in richness and contribution. The same can be said for the others mentioned in this chapter as they faced difficulties and then drew on their inner resources instead of being seduced by external rewards alone. They continually see possibility where others may see despair. They pick themselves up and do what they are meant to be doing with grace and wisdom.

The true prosperity of living from self-worth and for the highest goal makes every moment, but particularly the difficult ones, a chance for an inflection—a new tone, a curve up in your life, a shift to something greater that is your destiny.

Turn Your Fears into Breakthroughs

God grant me the serenity to accept the things I cannot change,
The courage to change the things I can
And the wisdom to know the difference.
Living one day at a time
Enjoying one moment at a time
Accepting hardships as the pathway to peace
—from the Serenity Prayer

YOU HAVE LIVED OUT THE BLESSING of the Serenity Prayer at times in your life. You became serene, had courage and drew upon your natural wisdom. You could do these things because you were present, and you walked into situations that tested you as part of your path to the highest goal.

Like most of us, you probably taste this peace only occasionally. Still, that means you know it. You'll begin to understand how you can have this experience all the time by facing the challenge of time and stress, which is the subject of this chapter. The grounding of the highest goal allows you to see your fears for what they are: information and energy you can learn from and turn into opportunities of the most lasting kind.

If you practiced the Do Only What You Love, Love Everything You Do live-with, you have already realized benefits from working on the prosperity challenge. Taking the time to do something you love—even in the face of a stressful deadline—enables you to do all things more easily and quickly. When you understand your inner qualities, you assign priorities in a new way and move more directly toward what is important to you.

Though you may already have changed your relationship to time and stress by working on your prosperity challenge, you will benefit still more if you go on. No challenge is isolated from any other. When you change your approach to one, you also change your needs with regard to others.

Stress and the Blessing of Fear

Fear lies at the heart of the time and stress challenge. Don't be embarrassed about having fears—that would be judgment judging the judgment. You, like all human beings, have hopes, visions and challenges; therefore, you worry and experience fear.

Fear is the sensation of "expectation with alarm," according to one dictionary definition. We associate it with an emotional and physical sensation. We relate to it less consciously than we could. Fear is inevitable and real, but the way we understand and react to it is not.

Consider fear a chance for another look at life. As author Melody Beattie says, "We need to learn that the gifts don't come when we get everything that we want, when we want it." Brother Wayne Teasdale says, "I think the other side of suffering is when you don't fight it. When you open up to it."

One Indian scripture, the *Spanda Karikas,* suggests that fear, like other strong emotions, is part of the throb or vibration of the universe: *spanda.* Follow any fear you have to its source, and you will find nothing but energy, an energy that you can tune into for the better. Fear comes from the same energy, the same universal vibration or *spanda,* as what are thought to be more positive emotions such as joy, hope and communion.

But fear gives us a greater blessing than these pleasant qualities because it indicates to us something that we need to do, something that we can learn from, something that can transport us to a new level of living. It constitutes the stuff of our tests. And if we confront any test that engenders fear, we can draw grace. As Eleanor Roosevelt said, "You gain strength, courage, and confidence by every experience in which you really stop to look fear in the face."[1]

People who accomplish what seem to be incredible tasks against terrific odds often don't see the risks they take. They have fears along the way, but their fears seem to push them to do even greater things with greater energy.

Chip Conley, for instance, founded a hotel chain and started a new concept in the hospitality industry by facing his fears. He opened the Phoenix Hotel in a very rough area of San Francisco at the age of twenty-six. He had no experience in the industry, and his friends and family thought he was crazy.

But his fears pushed him to innovate and take his own path. From the Phoenix, a legendary rock 'n' roll concept hotel, Conley created Joie de Vivre (joy of life) Hospitality, a chain of twenty-one boutique hotels, two day spas, and a coastal lodge and camp. And all of this resulted from his ability to tap the energy of his fears and turn them into breakthroughs, even during periods in which the hospitality industry experienced drastic cutbacks. He stayed true to his concept of honoring his people, keeping his organization open and creating successful niche-market hotels and other venues.

The saying "every stick has two ends" is apropos here. Every situation has an upside and downside, and the bigger the stick, the bigger the ends. The more you attempt, the more you achieve—and the more likely that you will be subject to stressors and fear.

Living More than a Good Life

Vice-Admiral James Stockdale and Jim Collins, both past speakers in the Stanford creativity course, walked across campus talking heatedly.

Stockdale, shot down on his second combat tour over North Vietnam, was the senior naval prisoner of war in Hanoi for eight years. He was tortured fifteen times, in leg irons for two years and in solitary confinement for four years. Yet he stood up for his beliefs, defied his captors and devised tapping techniques that allowed isolated POWs to communicate with each other.

Collins, author of *Good to Great: Why Some Companies Make the Leap . . . and Others Don't,* coauthor of *Built to Last: Successful Habits of Visionary Companies* and a lecturer at the Stanford business school at the time, was facing a difficult conflict with school administrators. He was trying to decide whether to confront people with his side of the situation or to leave without saying a word—the easier route because he had so many alternatives.

Stockdale said to Collins, "Look at those people we're passing here. They look fine. They don't look like they are in shackles. But they're all in their own prisons—prisons they construct in their minds." He went on to explain that these internal prisons stop us from doing what we know is right—from speaking up even when outer conditions seem to demand it.

Collins did speak up. In the process, he turned whatever fears he may have had into a positive inflection point in his life. Although he eventually left the university where he had had so much success, he created a dialogue that led to an openness that wasn't there before. And he felt great in the larger sense. His new life of contribution, achievement and joy was better than he could have imagined— greater than would have occurred had he stayed at the university.

You, too, come to points where you realize that you can follow the dictates of the culture that submerges you and live the good life, or you can find something more. Like a Stockdale or a Collins, you can live a great life—one that changes the world and the lives of those around you for the better. You can live from the highest goal.

None of this is possible unless you have integrity and take action on the basis of what you know to be true. And that is hard precisely because of the Voice of Judgment, or the VOJ—that internal critic that promotes the fears—stopping you from seeing the possibilities in your life.

You'll find that as you learn more about your Self and Work and apply them in the context of the highest goal, you'll be challenged and tested to live from them as opposed to the timid, safe, unloving, uncreative way your VOJ tells you to live. You can go, as Jim Collins puts it, from good to great.

Living in Self-Time

Most of us grapple with problems of time and stress because we are seldom present. We spend our time wandering through the vast repository of the past, with its memories, things we did wrong, people we liked and didn't like, and old loves. Guilt alternates with nostalgia for the good old days. When we look toward the future, we're filled with fear and anticipation of events that may never occur. The present hardly exists for us. Our minds dwell in these other modes, and we miss life.

Time isn't the problem; the way we approach it is. If we can stay focused in the present, in the eternal now, the grace of the present will open up possibilities for us. When we make the present all there is, the past and future—which are the dwelling places of the VOJ—become only tiny blips in our consciousness.

You have to decide whether you are going to live in VOJ-time or in Self-time. VOJ-time fills you with distractions: It leads to scarcity thinking, contracts your possibilities and allows your fears to loom large. You don't use your time wisely. When you live in Self-time, you intentionally stay in the present, drawing that intention naturally from your inner resources and your highest goal. Your intention honors time.

There's nothing mysterious about Self-time. You've experienced it when time seemed to expand, you focused effortlessly and you accomplished your tasks in a state of flow. You saw the world from the point of view of what you experienced, not what you were supposed to experience. In Self-time you naturally resonate with the highest goal.

How can you begin to live in Self-time? Try ignoring clocks or other timepieces for at least a day. Avoid radio or television reports that would give you the precise time. Tell people around you that you do not want to know the precise time. This isn't easy to do, especially if you try it during a workday, but the benefits can be great. When my wife Sarah did this for over a year, I watched her whole way of being open up. She still ignores precise time regularly, yet she accomplishes an amazing amount. Things seem to get done in the way they should get done.

Whenever I ignore clock time, I feel a similar opening. I pay more attention to the inner direction of my Essence than to the outer direction of timepieces and their accomplice, the VOJ. I get more done because, instead of making decisions based on clock time, I base decisions on how I actually feel and what I need to do.

Is there a task you regularly have to do but usually procrastinate about doing? You may be buffeted by the tyranny of the urgent, a fear that you can't get this task done or that you won't do a good job, or a sense that you can put it off to the last minute. Whatever the task, try accomplishing it by living in Self-time.

You don't have to completely ignore clocks to get into Self-time. Try setting a timer. Put it out of sight, and then just work without regard for how much time you are taking until the timer goes off.

I, for example, avoid writing. I can procrastinate about writing anything from books to emails, even though I know that once I get started I get completely absorbed and take just the right time for it. To combat my procrastination, I set a timer for three hours when I am writing material for a book. I can then focus totally on the writing instead of worrying about the time. Once I do this regularly for several days, I don't have to set the timer anymore. I just write until I know that it's time to do something else.

You can also get into the Self-time state by meditating and bringing that meditative experience into your day. Even if you experience this eternal time briefly each day, you'll notice a dramatic change in your relationship to time during the rest of the day.

Or you can try watching water. Spend at least half an hour watching water—the rain, a river, the ocean, a shower. Imagine living as water does—able to flow around things, having an inner power, being untamed. Then, for a day, live as water in everything you do.

You may be thinking that this is impractical: You have all kinds of pressures in your life. But try to move into Self-time. Bring your Self or Essence more into the world instead of being ruled by external measures. Experience the eternal now of Self-time at least once before we focus on fears and stress. Experiencing the eternal now is achieving the highest goal.

Transform Your Fears by Approaching Them

Now let's take a close look at fears. Using a sheet of paper, list fears that people have in general. Enjoy writing these fears and looking at them without identifying with them. Make as long a list as you can before you look at the list shown here. (A group generated this list in less than ten minutes.)

Which of the fears that appear on your list and the group list are fears you have from time to time? Circle or just mentally note those fears on both lists. Now look at your list and be ready to move a bit deeper.

SOME GENERAL FEARS

Abandonment	Failure	Spiders	Expenses	Illness
Death	Uncertainty	Inadequacy	Heights	Going gray
Earthquakes	Burnout	Dancing	Unknown	Suffocation
Humiliation	Commitment	New people	Change	Fear itself
Sagging	Dark	Being alone	Embarrassment	Mediocrity
Homelessness	IRS audit	Rejection	Mistakes	Dogs
Poverty	Going broke	Injury	Responsibility	Relocating
Drowning	Getting fat	Getting old	Success	Germs

[This list is intentionally in a random order.]

When you experience a fear, like the ones on your list, what do you do about it? The great psychoanalytical theorist Karen Horney identified three ways people deal with fear: move away from it, fight it or move toward it.

Most people move away from their fears—an act of denial or avoidance psychoanalysts call "repression." And the consequences of such a reaction can be neurosis or even psychosis. For most of us, however, repressed or avoided fears just never go away; they erupt in dysfunctional ways over and over again.

If you take the second approach, fighting the fear, you might overcome it in one area, but you likely won't get to the foundation of the fear. This is akin to trying to conquer fear of heights by doing parachute jumps. You may eventually be able to jump out of airplanes with relatively little fear and even exhilaration, but then you are invited to a friend's eleventh floor apartment and still find it difficult to step out onto the balcony. Why? Because the foundation of your fear of heights remains.

The third option is to move toward the fear. By approaching a fear, you get to know it and where it comes from. Observe the fear, stay with it and learn what the most appropriate reaction might be. When fear comes, what happens? Note your physical sensations. What can you learn from the fear? Observe it; it will normally disappear, and the mind becomes clear.

One of my students had taken flying lessons, but was often terrified when he was a passenger on a commercial flight that hit turbulent air—a metaphor for the tests we face in life. So he decided to move toward his fear. When turbulence hit, he paid close attention to what was happening within him and what was actually happening with the airplane. He realized that within him a disaster scenario was playing out. Of course, he knew that the odds were miniscule that a disaster would actually occur because of turbulence, but he noticed that he kicked into this mode whenever the plane got shaky. So he did something unusual for him. Instead of closing his eyes and gripping the armrests, he began to breathe deeply and pay attention to his breath. Then instead of giving in to the fear, he acknowledged it and paid attention to the turbulence itself. This pulled him away from his dysfunctional thoughts.

He noticed that the turbulence wasn't constant. It came in little spurts that normally fueled his fear but now just let him know—now that he was observing—that there really wasn't much going on. As he kept doing this on subsequent flights, turbulence became an opportunity to connect to his Essence.

You can take the same approach to the stressors in your life. Make a list of what is bothering you. The items on your list may range from small irritants to things that keep you up at night.

Consider which items on your list might be dealt with by immediate action and are essentially avoidable—things like paying bills or getting the car fixed.

See, however, that some stressors, such as those having to do with relationships (my boss is constantly criticizing me, my husband has lost his romantic side), don't just require action. They require new understanding. When stress comes from relationships, it's a mistake to ask an action question such as, "What should I do?" or even worse, "What do you think I should do?" In fact, you would be better off pausing and asking no questions, rather than asking these types of action questions. They limit your options—usually to what you've done before, which might not fit the current situation. Instead, try asking insight questions like the following. If you ask these questions in order and take time to be with each one—especially the one about intuitive wisdom—before you answer, you can get clear enough to know what action to take.

- For intellectual aspects, data and facts:
  What do I not yet understand?
- To get at emotional aspects:
  What is it I'm really feeling?
- For the physical senses dimensions:
  What do I not yet see?
- To get at your inner knowing:
  What does my intuitive wisdom say?
- To tap into your curious child aspect:
  What does the little kid in me have to say?

Finally, there are some stressors for which you can take no direct action, such as crime in the streets or a friend in the hospital with a terminal illness. For those you need to develop a new attitude. Any action—such as finding out more and talking about the crime problem or visiting with your friend—would have to be based on the highest goal in order for you to cope and develop something positive from the situation.

What Is Your Challenge?

I know what my time and stress challenge has been—I became aware of it from knowing my purpose and knowing who I am.

I tend to see many opportunities: I love to consider new possibilities. This sense of purpose can lead to overcommitting. Suddenly I reach the point where I can't really be present in the important aspects of my life. My personal side—my family, my spiritual work, my health and self-nurturing—suffer terribly. And I can't meet all my work responsibilities either.

Because at times in my life I had been successful working quickly under deadline pressure, I tended to let things go until the last minute, with the result being only a shadow of what I could have done. And that was painful to me. That pain, when I experienced it, was a tangible experience of my time and stress challenge.

I was like a compulsive gambler. I put out all these bets in the form of the commitments I made. I borrowed time from all sorts of sources, just like a compulsive gambler borrows money from the mob. And just like the mob, this challenge put tremendous pressure on me.

But by knowing my challenge well and using the highest goal to give me the perspective necessary to make choices, I have been able to turn this challenge around and make it work for me. You can do the same thing. Closely examine your personal challenges with time and stress, and you will know what to do.

Start by writing an initial statement of how time and stress impact your life. Does overcommitment lead to spreading yourself too thin in your professional and personal life? Do you waste time on trivial matters so you don't have time for the important things? Is procrastination your issue? What is your challenge?

When you've got a good idea of your particular challenge, ask yourself:

- What is the real issue, problem or obstacle underlying my time and stress challenge? What aspects of my personality lead to my time and stress challenge?
- If the truth were known, what are the decisions I regularly make that make things stressful?
- What are the patterns in my life story that have led to my particular issue with time and stress?

Now, before you go forward, try writing a vignette about your time and stress challenge. Or draw a picture of your fear connected with it.

Live-With:
Don't Worry, Just Do It

Perform this live-with for at least a week: Be open to possibilities, free from judgments of "wrong choices," free from fear of failure, free to live in the present moment and act from and toward your highest goal.

As you live this week with Don't Worry, Just Do It:

- Do face your fears and find their energy and teaching.
- Don't make yourself timid by worrying or agonizing over what might go wrong, is going wrong, has gone wrong, might have gone wrong, will go wrong, and so on.
- Do practice the Zen art of Being Here Now with a still mind, without chatter and seeing clearly.
- Don't worry about the future because God is already there.
- Do see yourself as the universal hero answering the call to adventure and leaping out of the "pit" of frustration and worry in all that you do this week.
- Do make a point of trusting that you will succeed in all that you do.

While you follow the admonitions of Bobby McFerrin and Nike, employ at least one of the following approaches:

Option 1: Practice emptying your mind so that it becomes free of the judgments and chatter that get in your way. Experience not thinking. Meditate regularly. Make notes about how you feel before and after each meditation. Notice how you approach things during the week, and see if you feel fears dropping away as you are more in touch with your highest goal.

Option 2: Set aside a half hour each day for worrying. During this half hour you can worry about anything you like. During the rest of the day, when a worry arises, simply tell it, "I'm sorry, but you're no longer allowed around at this time. You'll have to wait until my worry time." Then refuse to consider any worry until your worry time arrives. At worry time, really get into it. Worry as best you can for a half hour. You can keep a list of worries for your worry time, but forget them during the rest of the day. See if you can live every day practically worry free.

Option 3: Select a major task you have been anxious about or have been postponing for a while, and Don't Worry, Just Do It! Don't worry about messing it up; just start in on it and let it unfold for you.

Option 4: Keep a log of all the leaps of faith you make during the week. Big ones and little ones. Private ones and public ones. In what situations do you trust your Essence? And when are you a soul of little faith?

Option 5: Develop your own way of living with Don't Worry, Just Do It that fits your challenge and that works for you.

As always when you practice a live-with, be conscious of what happens. Take some time to write down what you learn, particularly when a fearful situation shifts into a breakthrough. Tell other people. Keep building on what works best for you.

Of all the live-withs, this one most often results in approaches that you can keep doing for the rest of your life. Much of this comes from the admonition to Just Do It. "I want to do this all the time!" enthused one practitioner. "It's so great. I've really enjoyed jumping on things that I've been putting off. Here are just a few examples: I wrote a deeply personal (and courageous) letter to a friend expressing some important feelings about a recent turn of events. I cleared my desk of a bunch of paper and other stuff from projects I'm not working on anymore. I filled out and mailed my application for a course that starts in a couple of months. I signed up for a weight-training program. There is more, but you get the idea . . . 'Just Do It' really inspires me."

Another participant made an important discovery about the power of this live-with: "I really need a few more weeks with this live-with . . . but then I guess I really have the rest of my life."

Most people living with this live-with find that the worry they generate about activities is worse than almost anything that could happen in those activities. That realization leads them to get into flow, without worry. And sometimes this live-with leads to profound discoveries about worries that have plagued people all their lives.

One woman faced the fact that she was constantly afraid that if she didn't achieve, "I'll be rejected. I'll be abandoned, fired, thrown away, discarded like the worthless garbage I really am." Then, as she contemplated that fear, she remembered a verse that says, "Perfect love casts out fear," and she was reconnected to her highest goal. She said, "The truth is, I am a unique and precious child of God, a woman of grace and courage, valuable because I'm here."

The Secret in Action:
Creating Your Own Culture

If you are conscious about your relationship with time and stress, if you do the practices suggested in this chapter, a shift will happen for you. You will be in Self-time, creating your own way of experiencing life without the restrictions of time. As you get into more situations of resonance with your highest goal, you'll be surprised how easy, effortless and enjoyable the flow of life will become.

If you experience a beneficial shift, even in a small way, don't stop. Your whole life can be like this, engaging the time and stress challenge in a way that is generative.

A friend of mine once told me about a woman from Thailand who entered his graduate program about twenty-five years ago when he was a student. She was fascinated by how busy people were in the United States. And then she realized that Americans were always trying to prove themselves. Americans would never stop being busy because they had to keep proving themselves—just like a football team that might win one Sunday but had to do it all over again the next week.

She found this strange and fascinating, because in Thailand (at least in the Thailand of her birth) people didn't have to prove themselves. Just the fact that they had taken a human incarnation meant that they were worthy of respect.

Now you can create your own culture, your own old Thailand, from the inside. Start doing things not for their external reward but because you love to do them. Seek no approval from others. Make no comparisons of yourself and your work to others. Don't worry about the future or have regrets about the past. Seek no recognition or reward. Work hard and do your best, for its own sake. Be the highest goal that you are.

Pay attention to your experiences as you live this way, even if you can do these things only part of the time. In this way, slowly build up your own culture of respect and faith in your inner resources and ability to stay on the path to the highest goal.

Stay with it so that you can bring the richness of your gifts to the world in time and with peace.

Relate from Your Heart

TAKE A MOMENT NOW to think about someone you love very much. This person could be living or dead, close to you or far away. But you love them deeply. Put that person in your mind's eye. Get a sense and an image of this person and feel the love that you have for them. Revel in that love as much as you want.

Holding and enjoying your love for this person, imagine that he or she has been away from you for a long time, but now is coming back to visit you. Because you have been apart, you are feeling the love you have even more intensely.

Imagine going to the airport and waiting for this person to come out of the arrival area. Experience this inside. Other passengers from the plane are coming out, and then you spot your loved one. You run together. You hug with abandon and feel the love pulsating between you. There is nothing else in the world but this moment. Feel the love in this moment.

Now drop the picture of the person and the airport scene, and continue to feel the love. Continue feeling the love as long as you can without the stimuli of the person and the airport scene in your mind.

You have just experienced your vast inner resource in the form of the love you have within you. When you experience this, you are experiencing the highest goal. This love doesn't come from the other person. It is within you. In fact, a great teacher once said, "There is enough love in the individual human heart to fill the universe."

Meeting the Relationship Challenge with the Highest Goal

When you relate with your heart, you understand that there is only one way to meet the challenge of relationships with the people in your world: the way of compassion—seeing the highest first in yourself and then in others.

A wide variety of people and traditions proclaim this truth. But it is not so easy to practice. Relationships test us—sooner or later, or maybe even multiple times each day. Know that these tests come to you in forms that are exactly right for you.

Just as with the time and stress challenge, you can learn to see relationship tests within the context of the highest goal: The love and compassion necessary to meet the relationship challenge are the embodiment of the highest goal, as well as the means for achieving it. When you experience love and compassion, you are touching the highest goal, enriching your relationships and making them the context in which you attain the highest goal.

Keep your highest goal in mind as you experienced it by thinking of someone you love. If you continue to see with your heart, to hold onto compassion, you can cherish the relationship tests that come in your life. If you pay attention to them, especially in this chapter's exploration of the Precise Observation practice, you'll learn a lot about yourself and be better for it.

Of course, we often don't express compassion in the way we should. We don't normally cherish difficulties and breakdowns in relationships: We get mad when a driver cuts us off, a waiter snubs us or our efforts go unrecognized by the boss or a coworker. Marriages suffer because couples seem to change after the ceremony. People who can't find The One stay single and worry about it. Some mothers are filled with guilt because they raised their voices to their children; others feel guilty because they didn't raise their voices when they feel they should have.

When we explore our fears in dealing with the time and stress challenge, we often find more secret fears in the relationship area than in any other. In addition, many of the fears related to other challenges also have a relationship component to them: "fear of not being able to maintain an earning level that will support a family" and "fear of not being able to cope with what is expected of me."

We secretly fear not being understood, being married, not being married, being alone or lonely, being hurt or rejected, not living up to others' expectations, being ridiculed, and not being able to love.

There are many ways to state the secret fears that go with relationships, but underlying all of them is a belief in duality and separation. This is a separation that even modern physics and systems theories don't support. If you can cast off the idea of separation from others and see the oneness and connection between all beings, then fears—all kinds of fears—can drop away. You can do this by relating from your heart and living a compassionate life with the support of the highest goal.

The Way of Compassion

An everyday lack of compassion thrives in our world. We are consumed with our own needs—we don't listen to others, we don't know what they need or how they live. We in the West don't bother to listen to people in other parts of the world. In fact, we rarely listen to our fellow citizens, our neighbors or our families. We don't even listen enough to ourselves.

And yet we have compassion inside of us. It comes out in extreme situations. Scott Morrison, who grew up in New Orleans, talks about how it appeared when devastating hurricanes approached the city:

> It was as if some silent, secret directive clicked in with every human being alive, overriding all other concerns and states of mind. Very clearly, it said: "Immediately drop whatever you are doing or thinking. Pay very close attention to whatever is happening. Be ready to help, if needed."
>
> . . . Suddenly, there were no Republicans and no Democrats, no Christians, Jews, agnostics or atheists, no gay people and no straight people, no blacks, whites, browns, blue-bloods or blue collars. No insiders or outsiders, no ugly people or beautiful people. Everything was just what it was, nothing less, nothing more, without labels or divisions. Everywhere, there was just the energy of clear, undistracted

attention and unreserved, unconditional care for everyone here.

What is possible in a hurricane or an earthquake, or a depression or any other kind of crisis, is possible at any time for virtually any human being who cares enough to stop the world. If we do so . . . we set into motion something that is without bounds or limits, something that will eventually touch everyone.[1]

To live as though you are truly alive and to have fulfilling relationships, you must develop the vision to relate from your heart in the present moment. Recognize that you—and everyone you interact with—have tremendous potential for greatness. Look for the good in yourself and everyone with whom you have relationships. Remember that all of us are constantly growing, expanding and evolving creatures.

When you see beyond and accept the façade of differences, you are closer to understanding others at their core and closer to making the kind of contribution needed from you in the world at this time. Living in this kind of compassion is living in the highest goal.

Live-With: See with Your Heart

It is only with the heart that one can see rightly;
what is essential is invisible to the eye.

Antoine de Saint-Exupéry,
The Little Prince

Sometimes we think of love as a special relationship reserved for our mate, parents or children. We think of it as a feeling that these select people elicit in us; therefore, when we don't have perfect relationships with them, we don't have love.

When you See with Your Heart, you practice Precise Observation: Your vision goes beyond what your eyes can know and is not clouded by your Voice of Judgment. You are able to see the best in people. This live-with is about living with compassion for yourself and others.

For at least a week, practice loving everyone you interact with (and even people you don't have direct contact with): associates, clients, friends, acquaintances, service people, other drivers, colleagues, even enemies. What I mean here by "loving" is appreciating the humanness of each individual by recognizing that each one has hopes, fears and personal dreams, just as do you. When you see the best in people, they tend to behave the way you see them.

Start close to home. Practice seeing yourself with your heart. Have faith in your creativity, suspend limiting judgments about yourself, and contemplate any resistance you might have to this. Most important, use the special form of precise observation you have when you See with Your Heart. What happens?

One man tried this live-with as he started to reorganize his troubled small business. He describes the impact it had on him and the people around him:

> One associate said that he just wanted me to know that, as he contemplated his responsibilities [as sole breadwinner for the family] for four teenage children, he was terrified not knowing how our adventure was going to turn out. He just wanted me to know that he needed my assurance that we were on the right path.

As I looked at him, I felt love for him and our work,
and said that I knew that our path . . . had heart and
we were drawn by love to the work we are doing and
whom we are serving.

All during the day as I worked with people, I felt
like the hole in the fabric of our functional activities
where the love of the Divine could pour through . . . I
sensed people to be more open to their creativity without
the fear holding them back. Open to the flow of the
Divine.

A woman who was practicing this live-with describes the outcome of one of those small incidents that can create major strain in relationships. She wanted to get home after a long day of shopping, but her husband wanted to explore one more store while she waited in their car.

Ten minutes passed, fifteen minutes. I started to get
impatient, then I remembered, "See with Your Heart."
I told myself, "He loves this place. I should let him enjoy
it, even if I have to wait." I waited forty-five minutes
and did not say a word when he turned up. He smiled
like a kid in a toyshop and I felt his joy.

Over and over again, in big and little situations, with close relations, with people on the street and with everyone in between, seeing with your heart leads to relating from your heart and toward moments of achieving the highest goal with others.

See what happens for you when you try it for a week. Or try it in a relationship that is critical for you. As always, keep some notes. Share your experience with others. Celebrate and build up your abilities for relationship in all parts of your life.

Listen

At an annual Systems Thinking Conference in San Francisco, the session on dialogue buzzed with conversation. The room was packed, and the crowd talked, laughed, and sometimes shouted at each other.

Suddenly the facilitator of the session, William Isaacs, author of *Dialogue and the Art of Thinking Together*, shouted out, *"Listen!"*

The people closest to him turned toward him with a bit of a startle. But not everybody paid attention, so the din continued, albeit at a somewhat reduced volume.

"Listen!" he shouted again. Almost everyone stopped talking and began sitting down.

"Listen!" he shouted for the third time to a now completely silent room. He had the room's full attention. Everyone was riveted, gazing at him in total silence. Then he read the following passage from the sage Krishnamurti:

> I do not know if you have ever examined how you listen, it doesn't matter to what, whether to a bird, to the wind in the leaves, to the rushing waters, or how you listen in a dialogue with yourself, to your conversation in various relationships with your intimate friends, your wife or husband . . .
>
> If we try to listen we find it extraordinarily difficult because we are always projecting our opinions

and ideas, our prejudices, our background, our incli-
nations, our impulses; when they dominate we
hardly listen at all to what is being said.
In that state there is no value at all. One listens
and therefore learns, only in a state of attention, a
state of silence, in which this whole background is in
abeyance, is quiet; then, it seems to me, it is possible
to communicate.
. . . [R]eal communication can take place only
where there is silence.[2]

Isaacs went on to explain that when we are in conversation,
like the people in the room before he started to shout, we normally
are not in silence in our heads. Therefore, we are not really listening to what is in front of us to perceive. As a wag once said,
"People don't listen. They reload."

One woman practiced seeing with her heart to listen to her
estranged daughter. She describes her experience:

*It was difficult. I kept falling back into my old defensive
ways. Well, it finally came to a head. She began to really
unleash some old anger, and I simply let go and let it
happen. I shut my mouth and my VOJ and really listened with all of my being. And as I did, she began to
change. She suddenly grew less defensive and began to
melt. I sat and let her feel what she needed to feel, and
say what she needed to say.*

> *. . . It felt so good for her to get this out. And it was*
> *such a clear moment for me . . . suddenly so much made*
> *sense.*

To try this for yourself, "Abide in silence," as one great teacher put it. See what happens as you quiet your mind. While you are listening to someone or something, get your mind silent by putting your subconscious attention on something else. You can repeat a mantra silently within. This is especially effective if you have had a practice of repeating a mantra. You can sense your arms and your legs, pay attention to your breath or silently do something repetitive such as moving a string of beads through your fingers.

Discover what works for you to silence your mind and become completely open to what is there, in the present. Remember that creativity is what happens between your thoughts. All the thinking you can do will not get you to solutions if you don't clearly perceive what is going on. When you experience that silence in an interaction with another, you are achieving the highest goal.

Community:
The Highest Goal in Working with Others

Outside conditions can force us to relate to each other in effective and loving ways. Any Midwesterner can tell stories of strangers helping strangers survive blizzards. People don't drive past cars and hapless drivers stuck in snowdrifts. Nor do they just use their cell phones to call a tow truck. They pull over, get out and push—working together to free the vehicle.

In situations like this, we act from a common goal and seem to be in flow. We see the best in others, and support growing and living in the highest goal. As in the storm-ready New Orleans of Scott Morrison's youth, people facing emergencies pull together, forget about differences, treat others with respect, and honor them for who they are. They act from a sense of connection and love. Even fear vanishes for the most part. All of this is living from the highest goal.

Sometimes the effect of a crisis lasts for years, erasing class differences and bringing new hope for solving problems. The crisis causes a shift in the system and in people's attitudes. The smaller goals and concerns and prejudices that people have give way to the highest goal of connection, compassion and creativity for all. This happened after the 1985 Mexico City earthquake and lasted well into the 1990s.

The same kind of beneficial shift often occurs in start-up organizations. With limited resources and people, but the possibility of great contribution to society, people work together without regard to hierarchy and written rules. Instead they operate with the highest goal implicit in everything they do. They work without thought of competition with others in the group and largely for the possibility of accomplishing something great despite their limited resources.

When I've taken the process described in this book of living from the highest goal to groups inside organizations, I've found that people start working together in this way. As individuals work on themselves, live with See with Your Heart and the other live-withs, and share their experiences, they get to know and respect each other. They trust each other, so they can be vulnerable and fight gracefully. When difficulties arise, the group works together to deal with them, and this creates a generative solution.

That way of working together is called "community," using the definition drawn from M. Scott Peck's book, *The Different Drum*. According to Peck, a community doesn't represent a group of people who live in the same town or go to the same church or school. A community forms and grows from the power of respect and trust in a group, just as our participants' work groups have.

This community embodies a quality of group interaction that goes beyond highly efficient teamwork, although it includes the best of what teams could be. It works in a creative way that supports the aspirations and development of the people in the group. It is inclusive and perceives everyone as a potential leader. It provides a safe place where people can make mistakes and be vulnerable without fear and with benefit to all. People communicate in an open and frank way and move toward consensus in making decisions. All types of love can flourish within communities of this type.

Like any profound relationship, community doesn't just appear out of thin air. Peck's Foundation for Community Encouragement, which offers community-building workshops, has identified four stages in groups moving toward community:

1. *pseudo-community,* in which people would be nice to each other, but not get below the surface;
2. *chaos,* in which people challenge and try to fix each other and there is a feeling of striving in the group;
3. *emptiness,* in which the pace slows and people begin to listen from their hearts; and
4. *community,* in which many—possibly all—of the characteristics of inclusiveness, diversity, leadership, trust, and so on, are operating.

You don't get to the community stage and then remain there forevermore. Groups or organizations move in and out of the four stages constantly. You must work to maintain community, especially as outer conditions change. Living with See with Your Heart can help you make choices together, deal with difficulties and sustain community, come what may.

The Committed Relationship and the Highest Goal

Marriage of any kind gives us tests (and grace) beyond any expectation. I've heard many stories of couples of all sexual orientations who had relationships for extended periods, even lived together, but as soon as they got married or pledged vows in a public ceremony, the relationship soured. The other person "completely changed." Sometimes the change occurred on the wedding day or even while preparing for the ceremony. The fact is, marriages or committed relationships continually give us tests that challenge and enrich our Self and bring out our best—if we accept these tests within the context of our quest for the highest goal.

There is only one reason to get married or enter into a public commitment with another: to go to God together. That reason reveals much about the relationship challenge, even if you replace the concept of God with another statement of the highest goal.

My wife, Sarah, and I are both in our second marriages; we have been together over twenty-five years. When we were dating, I remember sitting in her living room in Raytown, Missouri, saying, "Marriage is a crock. We'll never get married." Yet, eventually, we decided to get married—to go to God together. We realized each of us could help the other find our Self and be better people. In fact, though we didn't yet know the language of this book, we were finding our path toward the highest goal and dealing with our challenges together. Ram Dass's book *Grist for the Mill* supported us in pursuing this "conscious marriage." He wrote

> You'll find your way through this incarnation, each of us has a different path through. No path is any better than any other path. They are just different. You must honor your own path. For some of you, you will feel like half a being until you form a connection with another half and then you will be able to go to God. Others of you will go alone on your journey to God. It's not better or worse, it's just different. If you get over the value judgments, you can listen to what it is you need to do without getting caught in all of the social pressures about marriage or non-marriage. The true marriage is with God. The reason that you form a conscious marriage on the physical plane with a partner is in order to do the work of coming to God together. That is the only reason for marrying when you're conscious. The only reason. If you are marrying for economics, if you're marrying for passion, if you're marrying for romantic love, if you're marrying for convenience, if you're marrying for sexual gratification, it will pass and there is suffering. The only marriage contract that works is what the original contract was: We enter into this contract in order to come to God, together.

That's what a conscious marriage is about. In fact that is what everything you're doing is about.[3]

Sarah and I have found that having the highest goal for our marriage has not only helped us through the difficult times. It has also helped us turn those times into learning experiences and even breakthroughs. We are real partners on a quest. This vision, which we didn't have in our first marriages, has led us to the union we have now, the life we are leading now and the deep purpose we have for everything we do.

Interestingly, in the course of this journey together, there was no enmity for our former spouses. Instead, we felt gratitude and understanding. You don't have to go through suffering if you do everything, especially marriage, with a higher vision of what you can accomplish.

Forgive

As you live with See with Your Heart, you will inevitably get into situations in which you believe you are acting with compassion and others are not. They are not living for the highest goal but rather from the VOJ. They are not listening. They seem to be attacking you. They injure you in some way. They clearly are not relating to you with their hearts.

The cosmic sense would tell you that you are connected to others. There is no reason for anyone to wrong you because we are all one. But we all know how tests in relationships push us away from a recognition of oneness and love.

Consider these tests in relationships to be gifts—gifts that require you to find forgiveness through connection to your Self and the Self of others. Ultimately, you have to see things from the perspective of the highest goal in order to truly forgive.

You can make a beginning on this by seeing with your heart. Take any situation in your life in which you feel you need to forgive someone. Observe how seeing with your heart, with compassion, can help. Then consider how love and understanding can help you to forgive almost anyone.

When we lived with Forgive and explored forgiveness in our creativity-teaching group, we saw that the ultimate forgiveness is to forget, to see what has been done as part of a larger picture and to move on. Once we see that people often hurt us unintentionally, we can appreciate the flow of life of which each incident is a part and get on with living in the present.

The need to forgive on a day-to-day basis comes in many forms. People talked about needing to forgive a spouse or partner, someone honking at them at a traffic light, a person who raped them twenty-five years earlier, a family member who accused them of something, a person who bumped into them, a son or daughter who was unreasonably demanding.

We discovered that forgiving is a process, that it takes acceptance, communication and the connection that comes from seeing the larger picture. Often you have to take action. Sometimes you have to surrender with trust and faith. As one participant said,

The desire that emerges is to Forgive, and yet the feeling of emptiness, with nothing to stand on if I give up my anger, is so painful. No "platform," no "stage." To be in

the feelings of emptiness requires Faith on my part that
"this too shall pass," and it will morph into something else.

Know that the heart of forgiveness comes from connecting with your own heart in the way of compassion. Some people never surmount the difficulties of forgiveness in their lifetimes; others find forgiveness only when forced by stark circumstance.

One of the best illustrations of this truth can be found in Tolstoy's *War and Peace*. One of the novel's main characters, Prince Andrew, is a seemingly cold and calculating individual. He finds forgiveness on his deathbed, when, near his cot in a field hospital, he recognizes a wounded officer having his leg amputated as the man who ruined Andrew's relationship with the love of his life. Andrew remembers the first time he had laid eyes on his fiancée, and "love and tenderness for her, stronger and more vivid than ever, awoke in his soul."[4]

As Tolstoy put it, Andrew "now remembered the connection that existed between himself and this man who was dimly gazing at him through tears that filled his swollen eyes. He remembered everything, and ecstatic pity and love for that man overflowed his happy heart. Prince Andrew . . . wept tender loving tears for his fellow men, for himself, and for his own and their errors."[5]

As he lay dying over some weeks, Andrew reaches an epiphany:

Yes, a new happiness was revealed to me of which man cannot be deprived . . . happiness lying beyond material forces, outside the material influences that act on man—a happiness of the soul alone, the happiness of loving. . . . Yes—love. . . . But not love which loves for something, for some quality, for some purpose, or for some reason, but the love which I—while dying—first experienced when I saw my enemy and yet loved him. I experienced that feeling of love which is the very essence of the soul and does not require an object. Now again I feel that bliss. To love one's neighbors, to love one's enemies, to love everything, to love God in all his manifestations. It is possible to love someone dear to you with human love, but an enemy can only be loved by divine love. When loving with human love one may pass from love to hatred, but divine love cannot change. No, neither death nor anything else can destroy it. It is the very essence of the soul.[6]

As the literary scholar and yogi Harold Ferrar puts it, "Prince Andrew dies in complete peace. He has traveled the path of spiritual awareness from proud skepticism to indissoluble faith, and his life ends in absolute meaning. He finds not only happiness, but a kind of beatitude in embracing, in forgiveness and humility, the divine Presence within."[7]

You can follow this path too, not by dying but by bringing this deep kind of forgiveness into your relationships. Start right now by considering how Prince Andrew's story is mirrored in your own life. Have you forgiven an enemy? What led to your forgiveness? Do you have an enemy like this that you can forgive now? See what that may demand within you. Consider what gifts that may give you. Take some time to contemplate this, and then talk with a friend, perhaps someone you need to forgive, about it.

The Secret in Action:
Experience the Connection

At a meeting of the Presidio Dialogues, a monthly business-oriented conversation group in the San Francisco area, Michelle Newman, one of the participants, said she was experiencing a connection with everyone in the room. It felt to her as if we were all one and that we were working together. But before we got too arrogant about the group's connection, she mentioned that she often got that feeling in other situations, including rush-hour traffic. She described it as a sense that the traffic was moving in just the way it was supposed to move, almost like a dance. No matter how congested it was, she felt this connection and flow that was beyond words, a feeling of love.

Several of us said they had noticed this same phenomenon. When they saw traffic as a competition, with the other drivers preventing them from getting where they wanted to go, they experienced difficulty and disconnection. But when they felt the connection and saw their drive as a cooperative event, they got into flow and enjoyed it.

When you connect with others like this, you are resonating with the highest goal. You are fulfilling the purpose of your life. As you continue to live with See with Your Heart, keep noticing the moments of resonance that occur. Whether you are in a crisis at work, arguing with your significant other, dealing with family concerns, finding forgiveness, or stuck in traffic, remember that you can always experience, live with and move toward the highest goal.

Experience Synergy in Every Moment

Don't neglect your family! You can't afford to ignore your professional life! Don't take on too much! Stay active! Avoid stress! Balance your life! We get bombarded with advice from every quarter, telling us we must live happier, healthier, wealthier, saner, more balanced lives.

We know balance is important. We know that we can—and should—have rich, full personal lives and successful, satisfying professional lives if we just find the proper balance. But most of us don't know how to begin doing that, so instead we live with a vague sense that we are missing out. We get discouraged.

I suggest you ignore this background chatter about balancing your life. Instead, live with the truth that none of this really matters to you. Yes, the surrounding culture, friends, family, and colleagues can give you an idea of what's involved in living a balanced life, but you won't get anywhere until you discover what balance is for you and no one else.

When you say you want balance in your life, what do you mean? What is going on when you long for balance? Conversely, what is happening when you are satisfied with your life and don't even think of the balance challenge?

The discoveries you have made in previous chapters help you cope with the stresses of career, family and society; this chapter will help you develop balance among all of them. And the larger the perspective you develop, particularly if it is of the highest goal, the more you can experience synergy: the parts of your life working together to produce something more than their sum.

This synergy is beyond mere balance. You'll experience the energy of interaction in which your quest for the highest goal opens up your life in ways you never would have imagined. All of this is possible once you get into a flow of intuitive decision making, which links your highest capabilities with your practical daily issues.

Synergy, Not Balance

When Rochelle Myers and I were asked to do a weekend program in Oregon based on the course we had developed at Stanford, we pondered how to cram the material of a ten-week course into one weekend. We worried. Then Rochelle suggested we concentrate on the balance challenge because it brought together so much of what was important for people and drew on much of what we had discovered in our work. What's more, it offered the chance to bring the gift of intuition (that we all receive) to the context of real-life issues.

So we asked participants to think of a time when they had balance in their lives. We asked them to reexperience that time and tell us what it was like, what its conditions were and what led to the end of that period of balance. By doing this, we gathered data that made the weekend rich in discovery.

We expected that people would feel balanced when they had relatively little to do in their lives; so one finding, which we later replicated with other groups, stopped us in our tracks: Eighty-three percent of the people there said they experienced balance under busy, almost chaotic conditions.

We learned that people often experienced balance even as they were going through three or four stressors that should have put them at high risk for a heart attack (at least according to magazine quizzes that list stressors and caution you about not having too many of them). One man felt his life was in balance just after he finished graduate school and made a cross-country move with his pregnant wife. They were starting new jobs, moving into a new community and buying their first house.

What do you think accounts for balance in these sorts of conditions? As we talked to participants, a richer pattern emerged. For example, this man explained that he didn't have time to worry about little things. He just worked, spent time with his wife and did what needed to be done. He remembered being quite focused and enjoying everything he did. He and his wife felt closer than they had ever been. Even when they were apart, they felt that they were working on a mission together. A bond between them allowed them to get past the difficult issues and almost ignore the small ones. They were often astounded by what happened.

Descriptions like this are reminiscent of Silicon Valley start-ups in which a small band of people would work long hours, but almost not notice it because of the mission, energy and camaraderie that existed. In such start-ups, people often produce and create in amazing ways. A shared goal and the sense of a quest seem to push them to new heights that are, in a sense, addictive.

We decided that balance was the wrong word for what was going on here. While any one of these scenarios would seem to be enough to throw even the most stable individuals into a manic frenzy, people actually experiencing them seem to unearth inner resources and find clarity regarding their highest goal. It's almost as if these higher moments of intense focus prevent the VOJ and mind chatter from interfering.

When you're in such intense situations, you move into synergy, an experience of the highest goal. Usually you don't notice this state and don't realize it represents the highest goal. But if you can pay attention and remember the experience, you can turn your balance challenge into an opportunity to bring the highest goal into your life more consistently.

In any case, balance does not mean simply dividing your time and energy evenly between your work and personal lives. It means putting a large part of your energy into one part of your life, sometimes for rather long stretches of time. Balance is a synergistic and dynamic state of being that comes from your connection to the highest goal, not from external conditions or judgments. It requires finding time and energy not only for your family and profession, but also for your personal needs. As you integrate these parts of your life, this dynamic balance or synergy creates a focus and puts you into flow, a flow that nurtures you physically, emotionally and spiritually. It moves you toward the highest goal.

The Secret to Sustaining Synergistic Balance

Charles Garfield, a clinical professor of psychology at the University of California Medical Center, worked as a computer scientist for the Apollo 11 project that led to the first lunar landing. He says, "that technological achievement taught me a lot about our human capacity for inspired collaboration."

But that inspired collaboration, just like the synergistic balance of both individuals and start-up teams, came to an end. One day soon after billions of people around the world watched astronauts walk on the moon, Garfield went back to his desk at NASA and noticed that everything had changed. People were working, but there was no excitement. The inspiration and the synergy had vanished.

He asked his boss what had happened. His boss took him outside and pointed to the moon that could be seen faintly in the morning sky. "We don't have that to motivate us anymore," he explained.

When people told us about how their time of balance ended, they reported the same phenomenon: The reason for their focus and the synergy it produced disappeared. As their lives became compartmentalized and competing rather than energizing, work became just work, and "balance" became an issue.

Likewise, often after start-ups achieve a certain milestone, the work ethic and camaraderie don't have the same energy. As the start-up grows larger and turns into a full-fledged company, employees may work as much or even more, but they've lost their zest, so work interferes with other parts of their lives. They begin to feel out of balance.

This cycle of moving out of dynamic balance is not inevitable, however. While it is rare, some people and organizations maintain synergy and balance over relatively long periods of time. What is their secret? Some repeatedly create new visions that enliven their lives with synergy for a time. But only if a sense of the highest goal underlies those visions can a dynamic balance be maintained through all kinds of situations and synergy experienced in every moment.

Steve Jobs had a vision in the early days of Apple Computer, and he continues to move people with his vision. He visited our creativity class when Apple was a two-hundred-million-dollar company, which was impressive for its age. But he felt that a big part of his job was not letting his people get too complacent. He led them to a kind of synergistic balance (even though their lives often seemed to be out of balance in the short term) with sparkling visions of what the personal computer meant to the world. Underlying it all was something akin to the highest goal: He felt that people wanted an opportunity to express some deep feeling about contributing to society.

In my own case, I remember a period of balance that extended over two years and coincided with life-changing events that are playing out to this day. On reflection, I can see now that the focus and spaciousness I experienced during that time came from a pursuit of the highest goal. I had hit a low point in my life and rigorously set out on a search to find myself. I saw that the goals of achievement and financial rewards that had been so important to me were causing the difficulties in my life. I had been ever so effectively sub-optimizing, and it was leading nowhere. My search led to the highest goal in the form of the communion I experienced with a higher aspect of others and myself. This gave me a sense of purpose that frequently brought synergy into my life. I was fully present with a sense of love and light no matter what I was doing. I didn't feel any stress for long periods of time, and when I did, it dissipated quickly in the face of my sense of connection to and movement toward something greater.

This was not a time that was particularly easy for me on the surface of things. I was engaged in a rigorous inner search in addition to all the things I normally did. I was teaching one of the most difficult courses I have ever taught, consulting actively, writing, and dealing with gut-wrenching issues from my recent divorce.

But the experience and commitment to the highest goal allowed me to do all of this in a way that produced connection and a sense of well-being. And that commitment has sustained synergistic balance to this day through all the changes in my life.

This commitment to the highest goal is the secret to sustaining synergistic balance in your life. But that isn't enough. You must establish priorities and get into a flow of intuitive decision making.

Setting the Highest Priorities

When we're in synergistic balance, we operate in the eye of the hurricane, so to speak, finding our place of peace and making time to be with others, as well as with ourselves. In this point of dynamic equilibrium, you create meaning and get in touch with your own personal power. In fact, when you use that power intentionally, you can experience this synergy and resonate with the highest goal.

How can you get into and stay in this state in a way that is right for you? First, set priorities from a clear sense of who you are at core, your life purpose and the highest goal. You can't have dynamic balance based on someone else's dharma or life purpose. And you can't achieve this beneficial synergy if you don't turn your needs into priorities.

Consider one professor's demonstration of balance: He began by filling a large glass container with rocks. When it seemed as though the jar was filled, he asked the class, "Is this jar full?" The class nodded in agreement. He then poured pebbles into the jar, which filled in the empty spaces. He then asked the class, "Is the jar full now?" They agreed that there was no more space in the jar. He then poured some sand into the jar and asked the same question. The class, a bit cautious in replying, said, "Yes, there is no way that anything else can fit in that jar." The professor then poured some water into the jar until it reached the top. The jar was indeed now filled to its maximum capacity.

The professor demonstrated something profound about how you can achieve balance: The rocks represent the big issues in your life. If you don't put them in first, you can become overwhelmed by the smaller but pressing issues represented by the pebbles, sand and water. Your life will have lost its meaning and zest because you never get to the big issues.

Exploring Your Balance Challenge

Look at the 2×2 table shown here, which condenses the balance issue to two questions: Do you feel you are doing well or poorly on the professional side of your life? Do you feel you are doing well or poorly on the personal side of your life? If you fall in the upper left cell, you consider both parts of your life are going poorly. If both parts of your life are going well, you're in the lower right corner. And

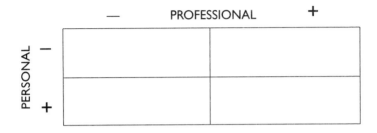

if you're in one of the other two corners, one aspect of your life is going well and the other poorly.

Take some time now to consider where you would put your current life situation in that empty table. You can learn something about the nature of your balance challenge by deciding how you feel about current conditions. Once you put yourself in one of the quadrants, think more about why you put yourself in that quadrant.

Often if you dig deeply, you'll get an insight on your balance challenge. When I do this exercise with MBA students, I expect them to be largely in the upper-right quadrant with strong professional life and weak or poor personal life. But when I did this recently with a group of forty MBA students, more than forty percent of them felt that both their personal and professional lives were going well; just twenty-three percent fell in the quadrant I expected to have the largest group.

When I talked to them individually, we got into the kind of depth I'm hoping you can derive from this exercise. One woman, surprised to find herself in the lower-right corner of the table, realized her definition of balance led her there. She had had the benefit of working with a female mentor in a New York investment bank.

This investment banker, a mother of three and head of a global group within the bank, had let her in on a little secret: "If you try to achieve balance on a daily basis—forget about it!" she told the student. "You have to look at it over a longer horizon."

The student realized the wisdom of this view. It not only alleviated her frustration when she needed to dedicate large chunks of time solely to work, it also relieved guilt associated with devoting days or weeks to her personal life. "Over time," she said, "I have adequately tended to both and have therefore managed to, on average, achieve balance."

She made another important discovery: "Balance is dynamic—not static. It is not elusive, but somewhat fleeting." That's why the quest to achieve and maintain balance is one of life's greatest challenges.

No matter where you feel you are on the table, use it to ponder the nature of your balance challenge. What part of your life seems to give you the most trouble? Think about how you feel about balance. How do you feel when you are in a state of synergy? What conditions led to that state? What did it feel like physically, spiritually and emotionally? What is stopping you from experiencing that balanced state of synergy more often? How does the highest goal, as you know it, enter into your sense of balance?

Take some time to mull over these questions. Talk to others about them. Write some notes that will help you celebrate synergy as you've known it, and use that experience to consider your balance challenge now.

Another woman considering her balance challenge put it very simply:

I hate the life-maintenance stuff. I pay bills in bursts, respond to deadlines last moment. My creativity works the same way. What upsets my balance is when I not only put things off, but also let them nag me.

She began to realize that she needed to face a balance-maintaining "yes/no" and "now/later." That meant, she realized, "I have to do at least some of the creepy stuff *now*." But it also meant that when she could do it later, she needed to put it away until then. She determined to give herself permission to say, "It doesn't make sense to think about this now—either do it or don't."

When you understand your balance challenge, you begin to get a solution for it, especially when you are willing to make decisions such as the "now/later" ones this woman used. She decided to do a little extra homework up front and to acquire two habits: She wrote reminder markers in a calendar and looked at that calendar everyday. Now she knows she can safely let herself be carried away when the creative juices are flowing—"until I stub my toe on one of the little markers I'm remembering to place in my path. It's simple. It's my friend and it helps me balance. It seems to be working."

A management consultant discovered that her balance challenge intensified when she felt saddled with a lot of "should do" feelings rather than "want to do." That's what made her feel "out of control of my life, as though I am not living it for me but for some other person or purpose that isn't consistent with my Self and what I want to be doing."

Can you see how having a highest goal can help her with her balance challenge? By bowing to the pressure of "should do's" she is sub-optimizing. If she lived with the highest goal, there would be no "shoulds" in her life, only what came naturally on her quest.

She discovered this for herself as she worked on a mosaic tile project for our creativity class. She concentrated on connecting with her Essence quality of contentment (which includes the qualities of calm, patience, renewal, quiet, serenity, simplicity, tranquillity, and wholeness). "I just did what came naturally," she explained. " I made a conscious decision not to spend time deliberating and second-guessing myself about the perfect mosaic design, and instead just to dive in and make quick, intuitive decisions as I went."

When she lived in the highest goal by drawing on the qualities of her Essence, the "shoulds" lost their power to pressure and pull. She found balance.

Notice that she experienced synergy with her highest goal of contentment when she made "quick, intuitive decisions" as she worked. For all of these course participants, their decision to make choices allowed synergy to appear, and the balance challenge turned into a way of living from the highest. Keep this in mind as you flesh out your own balance challenge and use your highest goal to give you direction along the way.

Get into a Flow of Intuitive Decision Making

You don't develop a balanced, dynamic life by theorizing, but by making decisions day by day, minute by minute, from an intuitive sense of what is right for you. You may find this difficult because the accepted way to make choices—coupled with your own habits and VOJ—stops you from making decisions efficiently. Most of us tend to make decisions either emotionally or with compulsive "analysis paralysis" rather than relying on our inner gift of intuitive knowing.

Beth Sawi, a retired Charles Schwab chief administrative officer and author of *Coming Up for Air*, told my class about how we make balance decisions almost by default. Her scenario: As you are about to leave for work one morning, your daughter says that she needs to talk to you. More than likely, you would say a few words, and then, since you need to get to work, suggest that the two of you complete the conversation later. But, let's say at the end of your business day, your boss says he needs about an hour to work with you before you go home. You would probably stay without thinking about it.

To what extent do the different ways you might treat these two situations come from an obligatory response, rather than what you really want? Sawi's point is that in order to achieve any kind of balance in our lives, we need to get off automatic pilot and make choices on the basis of what is important to us.

So the solution to your balance challenge is to get into the flow of intuitive decision making. By practicing observation and asking penetrating questions, you can hear what your inner intuitive voice has to say. Instead of agonizing over each decision and how it affects your ability to have balance ("Should I work late or go home? If I go home, should we eat out or stay at home? If we go out, which restaurant should we go to?"), listen to your inner intuitive voice, which comes to you as a sense of rightness rather than emotion or desire.

We are taught to make decisions analytically. We are persuaded that intuition is the soft, emotional way; it's the province of people who mean well, but don't possess the intellectual skills necessary for making hard decisions. Quite to the contrary, intuition is a powerful resource that we all have, but we must develop it.

It's not necessary to abandon facts or lose the ability to analyze to use intuition; it complements reason. Despite what most people think, intuition is unemotional. It is an inner knowing beyond and deeper than emotions. But it demands action: You develop your ability to connect with and use your intuition by acting on it and seeing the results. When you do that over time, you understand that intuition is mistake free, and you will be able to explain your intuitive decisions to others using hard facts and results.

When you don't use your intuition, you get lost in a quagmire of indecision. When you live from intuition, you achieve the highest goal in each moment.

Live-With: Yes or No?

So get started right now. Face your balance challenge with questions and choices from your intuition. Live with Yes or No? to get at your intuitive power. For at least a week, every time you have a decision to make, ask if it's a yes or a no to explore the decision within you at all times. Your Essence is always ready to do what is appropriate—particularly with decisions that affect the interface of your personal and professional lives.

To do this, start small. Pay particular attention to personal decisions in narrow areas. How do you typically make such decisions? What patterns have you followed until now? Do you have difficulty making the big decisions or the small ones? What situations or people throw you off your intuitive power? See that you may be fighting the fear of making wrong decisions and displeasing others. There is no better tool to fight that fear than your faith and understanding of your highest goal.

This live-with will work for you only if you are willing to let go of standard ways of making decisions. It involves no lists, no conclusions, no weighing of sides, no logical deductions. It involves action.

Start by making all of your daily mundane decisions on an intuitive yes/no basis during the week with this live-with. Acknowledge that everything in life is a yes or no and that you always have a decision within you. Try this: Focus on a decision that you would like to make, perhaps something you have put off dealing with or perhaps a decision you need to make today. Make a commitment to abide by whatever decision this exercise picks.

Now get a coin and assign one side of the decision (Yes or No, Alternative 1 or 2, Now or Later) to heads and one to tails. Now flip the coin.

How do you feel about the outcome? Do you feel great that this is the right outcome? Or do you want to do two out of three flips? Your feeling, coming from inner knowing, tells you what decision you have within you already.

You can use this exercise throughout the day, every time you need to make a decision. Whether it's to wash your hair, send a thank-you note or go out for dinner, use a coin to find your intuitive decision, act on it and see what happens to support your intuition. During the week or so that you do this live-with, make at least one major decision (buy a new car, quit your job, take a vacation) on an intuitive yes/no basis.

When you use the coin flip, you'll see that the second you flip the coin, your gut instinct reacts one way or the other. Intuitively, the answer already existed within. Eventually, the coin-flip exercise can become so natural that you don't have to use a coin to see your answer. After a while, you don't even have to think about the coin; you just start making decisions intuitively.

Find a way to spend some time alone this week—a necessary condition at the start for listening to your intuition. Turn off your car radio. Take walks by yourself. Find a quiet and solitary place to work. Screen your phone calls and return only those that are really important. Meditate. Do whatever works for you. The trick is to find ways to integrate intuitive decision making into your life. Time alone is necessary for creativity and intuitive inspiration.

Decisions don't always need to be acted upon. What's important is that you know what the truth is—for yourself. For example, you might ask, "Is it yes or no for me to take care of my sick father?" In truth, your answer may be no, and you may then follow it with another question: "Can I live comfortably with that decision?" If the answer is no, then go in search of a creative solution that serves both you and your father. If the answer is yes, you may still need to provide for your father in some other way.

This process allows you to see your underlying issues—in contrast to the business-as-usual approach of refusing to allow such questions to be raised at all. When you refuse to look at them, they may be replaced by VOJ statements: "You should take care of your father." "You are terrible for not wanting to," and on and on. This blocks all possibility for (1) knowing the truth, (2) accepting the situation, (3) going in search of a new solution, and/or (4) completing what needs completion. If there is no blockage, you can handle a potentially complex situation in a direct and straightforward manner.

A Life of Choice and Balance

Many of the alumni of the creativity course have grabbed on to the Yes/No live-with and used it throughout their lives. Few have done this with the consistency of Heidi Roizen, now managing partner of Mobius Venture Capital.

Heidi was the first alum of the creativity course to come back as a speaker. In 1985, about two years after graduating from our MBA program, she came back to demonstrate a drawing program called ClickArt that she had developed for the new Mac computer. The students were going to use her program to draw mandalas on the computer. Instead, the class, some of them older than Heidi, became fascinated by what she was saying, and she became more important than the computer.

When we talked about her balance challenge at that time, she said it was no challenge for her because all she was doing as the CEO of a start-up was working. She had nothing to balance.

But that changed. She got married, had two daughters and a strong family and community life. After building her company to fifteen million dollars in revenues and selling it, she joined Apple Computer as vice president of Worldwide Developer Relations in perhaps the most tumultuous times of that company's history. She had a three-hundred person group that dealt with some twelve thousand developers. She did well but decided to leave because she could see that the situation was getting her life out of balance. She really couldn't be with her daughters or support her husband.

At the time, she received a lot of criticism for quitting. *USA Today* essentially blamed her for the fall of Apple, "and I laughed," she recalled. "I didn't get bent out of shape about it because anyone who knows me knows that such a statement was ridiculous. For most people, to be singled out by a national newspaper as the cause of a company's failure would be a major career blow. But for me, it didn't really phase me."[1]

What is it that keeps her going through all this into an experience of synergy in her life? Her highest goal of connection with her inner resources and her partnership with her husband and daughters provide her anchor. She says,

> I believe in living my work life in stages, and I still consider myself to be in my wage earning years . . . [at the same time] . . . The value that I would like to continue to provide for my husband, first and foremost, is to love him, to respect him, to trust him completely and to be completely trustworthy to him. We call our home our sanctuary. Our partnership is sacred to us. Pretty corny stuff, but so important to me. . . . For my kids, the story is somewhat similar. Love, trust, feeling of safety at home.[2]

Another source of her strength comes from the Yes/No live-with she developed from the creativity course. She says, "There have been many times in my life when I've found myself overanalyzing an issue, and I've stepped back and said, 'Is it a yes, or is it a no?' I rely on that technique a lot."[3]

Heidi has been named to the list of the hundred most influential people in the microcomputer industry. She's been the president of the Software Publisher's Association, a public governor of the Pacific Exchange and a board member of the National Venture Capital Association as well as several corporations. In all these situations she brings the synergy of her highest goal and the clarity of her sense of balance in mentoring and supporting others from a sense of the sacred. She says,

> At the close of my life, I'd like to look back and know that I got—and delivered—good value out of living. I'd like to know that I took advantage of the opportunities that I was blessed with for myself and my family. I want to know that I created good balance in my life, enjoyed it, lived well, and enhanced the lives of others in the process.[4]

The Secret in Action:
Living in Synergy with the Highest

The Yes or No? live-with, then, is really about telling yourself the truth and trusting your Essence to communicate that truthful message to you so that you can live in the synergy of the highest goal. If you do this consistently and pay attention to the results, you'll live in a flow of intuitive decision making.

The state of synergy in every moment almost defies description. Deepak Chopra alludes to it in his book title, *The Spontaneous Fulfillment of Desire*. A more textured view comes from a Sufi tradition that says that the Essence quality of Joy has the slogan, "I wish," meaning, I think, that this joy is a dynamic quality. You wish for something inside, from a place of connection to the highest goal, and you get it . . . immediately! And the experience of this constant wishing/fulfillment is joy as well as the experience of synergy.

That's what this flow is about. Eventually you realize that connecting with intuitive wisdom is not just connecting with something inside of you, it is connecting with the highest. A legal specialist who did the Yes or No? live-with got into intervals of synergistic flow. When this happened, she said, she was reminded of her grandmother's favorite saying: "God's plan works. Yours doesn't."

Eventually you realize that you aren't *doing* anything. Sure, you have intentions and you try to deal with the tests life throws at you. But when you live from the highest goal, you are connected to a higher power. It's like hearing a voice each day that says, "Good morning! This is God speaking. Don't worry. I'll take care of everything for you today. I don't need any help. Have a nice day!"

It's hard to keep this in mind when we come to difficult times, but it helps to see those dry periods or "pits" as part of the hero's journey, part of God's plan and a manifestation of the highest goal.

Gale D. Webbe described the sacred nature of these dry periods in *The Night and Nothing*:

> Spiritual dryness, if that is God's will at the moment, is as much to be loved and obeyed as spiritual fervor. It takes repeated aridity to bring home to us that our own so precious feelings contribute nothing to our salvation; that, in fact, they generally stand in the

way of our perfection. Spiritual dryness can finally lead us, after much pouting, actually to give thanks that it is not because we see God that we have joy. It is because [God] sees us.[5]

Know that when the balance challenge pushes you to live from the highest goal and connect with your intuitive wisdom to create moments of synergy, you set a force going that changes your life. You get into a generative state. And you can spread that state to others. How you can do that is the subject of the next chapter.

Become a Generative
Leader

I BEGAN THE JOURNEY of writing this book because I realized that something unexpected was happening to people who took our creativity course at Stanford and elsewhere: People who have been through the course seem to blossom, to access some secret source of energy and inspiration. They find new ways to contribute to their organizations, participate in their communities and bring love and energy to their families and friends. They thrive on diversity, fight gracefully and treat others with compassion, acceptance, appreciation, and respect. They go through a transformation that starts with the course and grows as they face life challenges and apply course ideas.

You know now what was happening. Specifically, these people shifted their priorities in life toward the highest goal. They achieved success in normal terms, but they went beyond that. Their quest to experience the highest goal, no matter how they define it, sustains them and energizes them for the tough times. And they can go back to live-withs and other approaches that are found in this book when they run into difficulties or just want to expand their ability to connect with the highest goal.

The Ultimate Challenge

But there is more—another challenge that keeps the quest for the highest goal alive and brings your individual work into the world. This is the ultimate challenge of sharing your gifts, of bringing your inner resources, your highest Self, out into the world for others. Unless you can find a way to do this at some level, you haven't really achieved the highest goal.

As you find a way to do this, you begin to receive from others and the universe. As you give and receive, you get into a larger flow than just the flow of absorption in the moment. This flow goes two ways rather than one. Your inner resources connect with the systems around you, and at the same time, these systems nurture you. Your quest for the highest goal is fed in a natural way because being in this flow is the highest goal itself.

The challenge comes from not seeing the gifts you have in your life. If you don't appreciate your gifts, you won't see the opportunity to give—nor will you see the gifts that come your way. You may have a sense of scarcity that leads you to believe you must hold on to what you have: If you let go, you think, all will be lost. Sometimes a test makes it almost impossible for you to see the underlying gift and stay in the flow. A job is lost or a relationship breaks down, and you're more likely to perceive an ill wind roaring through your life than the gift being offered to you.

Yet some people don't let expectations get in the way of giving and receiving. They give of themselves and realize they are getting a lot in return, even if it isn't what they expected. The graduates of our courses and offerings repeatedly show, by their life experiences, that it is possible to face obstacles, get into the flow of giving and receiving and become more than leaders. They become generative leaders.

Becoming a Generative Leader

You've read about many of our graduates who have taken this extra step into generative leadership: Denise Brosseau, who changed the game for women entrepreneurs by helping them find funding and develop networks; Jeff Skoll, who turned his fortune into investing in, connecting and celebrating social entrepreneurs; Julia Romaine, who specializes in leadership work with corporations and created a successful, continuing creativity program for the families of the victims of 9/11; and Jim Collins, who has fashioned a life that is purely his own and become a top thought leader in the business world.

These people (and others whose stories you've read here) are generative leaders: They create creativity. They have discovered the secret of how to give and receive in an endless cycle of renewal.

Consider the way in which a natural system regenerates itself. In a rain forest, for example, every living organism contributes to the ecosystem. Barring human interference, the rain forest is regenerative. It never depletes its resources because every creature and every bit of vegetation contributes to the system; the forest recycles and flourishes on its own waste products. God has given us this model and this gift.

When you are generative, you contribute to this cycle of renewal. Your synergy, something more than the sum of its parts, starts a positive spiral of intelligent growth. This is what life is all about: It is living with the highest goal.

To be of service and make the contribution only you can make to the universe, you must become a generative leader—no matter what your role in life. You can be a leader to yourself, to one other person or to the world. But if you start right now with an intention of being generative, of letting your creativity create creativity around you, of giving and receiving, you'll see remarkable things happen.

One Generative Leader

It's not always easy. Take the case of Joe Tye. Joe was co-president of his Stanford MBA class when he took the personal creativity course. Then he became passionate about a cause, and his journey took a sharp turn from the typical MBA career path.

In conducting research for another course, he concluded that the tobacco industry promoted smoking to young people, and he wanted to do something about it. He formed Stop Teenage Addiction to Tobacco, or STAT (a word that means "quickly" in the medical world) to counteract the industry's messages. STAT played a key role in initiatives to prevent the sale of tobacco to minors and raised awareness of tobacco industry efforts to promote nicotine addiction, especially advertising that encouraged children to smoke and discouraged adults from quitting.

Though the organization made an impact, Joe wasn't earning the income of a typical Stanford graduate. In fact, he and his wife and two children were living in a trailer at one point. So he returned to his past profession of hospital administration and became chief operating officer of a major teaching hospital while he carried on his fight against teenage smoking.

As he continued to follow his own path, he started writing about his experiences. He became a consultant, speaker and author, teaching values-based life and leadership skills in all sorts of settings. He has written and produced more than a dozen books and tapes on personal and organizational success, including *Never Fear, Never Quit; Your Dreams Are Too Small;* and *Personal Best.*

He works with organizations to cultivate more positive and productive workplaces and with individuals to help them achieve their goals by living their values. His material is based in the highest goal and couched in language that moves people to change their lives.

Joe is a generative leader. He says,

The Personal Creativity in Business class was by far the single most influential course I have ever taken. Among the many benefits I derived were first, the philosophical principles that we covered were vital in my own decisions to give myself permission to follow a nontraditional path in life; second, whenever I have run into roadblocks in life or in business, I've fallen back on the practical strategies we learned in the class . . .

His highest goal is to live with all the potential that God has given him. As he follows this path, he has discovered a paradox: He can approach this goal only by helping other people become who they are meant to be. "The more I focus on myself and my own goals, the less authentic I am, and the farther I am from the person I am meant to be," he observes.

The words of Confucius guide him, he says, quoting *The Analects*: "You yourself desire rank and standing; then help others to get rank and standing. You want to turn your own merits to account; then help others to turn theirs to account."

Live-With:
Participate in the Flow of Giving and Receiving

Joe has discovered a powerful live-with: Participate in the Flow of Giving and Receiving. Following in the footsteps of a long tradition of generative leaders, he experiences the highest goal when he gives help to others, receiving back in quantity and quality more than he could possibly imagine.

You, too, can use this live-with to carry you into a life as a generative leader. Take some time, preferably as much as a week, to Participate in the Flow of Giving and Receiving. Pay attention to what happens. You will see that your acts of giving and receiving become generative and show you how to lead in that way.

Please start by considering your own experience with giving. Are you giving from the deepest part of yourself, or are you pushed by VOJ or self-interest? How have you been generous in the past? What happened? In what situations have you pulled back from giving when you could have given? What does it mean to be giving and generous? How can you open up to giving more of your Self, your gifts, your Essence, and your Work to others and to yourself? How have you experienced the highest goal when you gave?

Then try to put your challenge with giving and receiving into a sentence. Maybe you have a scarcity attitude. Perhaps you don't want to share because you feel others should work harder to get what you have created. Or maybe time and stress holds you back. Maybe the VOJ is saying something that is stopping you. Or perhaps you never notice what you get back when you give.

Attack your challenge by getting into the flow of giving and receiving. Give in at least one situation, especially in one in which it is difficult for you to give. Perhaps you can give something that you have been holding off giving. Give of your Self when you give. Feel the energy of giving. Give when it is difficult to give. And in all giving, give your inherent gifts, your Self and your Work.

As part of this live-with, give blessings to others. By doing so, you are subtly acknowledging the highest goal, because only one who is worthy and connected to the highest can bless others. Try it. Start your blessing with, "May you . . ." and finish it with something that comes from the heart. Sometimes this simplest thing can open up the one blessed and the one blessing to something greater than either could imagine, as the experience of one person living with this live-with illustrates:

> *I was sitting on a bench looking out at the Claremont Hotel, sipping my tea and reading. A man asked if he could share the bench and I said of course. We sat there for quite a while, each of us reading in silence. Then this man sneezed. I said, "Bless you." He responded with, "Thank you. We all need all the blessings we can get." When he said this, I remembered the live-with and how important it is for each of us to give blessings . . . that it is something each of us can do so easily, and yet it is so very powerful. So I responded, "And how easy it*

is for us to give them." He turned and looked at me and smiled.

We then began an incredible conversation. . . . He had just arrived from Shanghai where he was on a business trip. He was due to return to Washington, D.C. We spoke about the world situation, his travels, our interests, work (including Creativity in Business and my plans for teaching it), and then our conversation turned to our families.

As we shared details about our families and life experiences, we began to share more intimate stories. This man had a child who had suffered as an infant from a virus that affected her heart and her brain. He suddenly grew very quiet, and then, as tears began to form in his eyes, he shared his deepest fears about her life and how he worried he would not be there for her. When he was done, he looked at me and thanked me and told me, "It is so easy to talk to you because you are so present and giving of yourself. You really care. Your eyes shine with love. You will be very good at this work." I was so touched by his openness and honesty. We both cried and then shared a long hug and blessings. We then said good-bye.

I was so taken by the fact that a simple blessing and my complete presence to him and his feelings could open up to a deeply memorable experience for both of us. And while I will most likely never see him again, I will remember him sharing such intimate feelings with me, as well as his affirmation to me that I am where I need to be right now. We were both very present with each other, listening with all our beings, and therefore, able to truly give and receive gifts of Grace.

As you give, also be open to gifts you receive. Recognize the present of the present, the grace that often happens without your notice and what comes from people who don't really have a lot to give materially. Put your conscious intention into living each day with a sense of generosity and receptivity. Take note of:

- What do you do?
- How do you feel?
- What supports your sharing and generosity?
- What closes it down?

Here are some additional suggestions to put in practice during the week you do this live-with:

- Find a way everyday to give generously to your Self. Ask yourself each morning, "What gift can I give to myself today?"
- Find a way to surprise someone in your life— especially strangers—with a gift daily.
- Give without the receiver knowing you are giving.

As always with live-withs, keep a record of your experiences. Make some notes. Contemplate what happened, and look for generative experiences. Talk to other people about what happened, and participate in the flow of giving and receiving in your conversations. Celebrate your breakthroughs, and keep applying what you learn.

Once again, you can experience this live-with on several levels. Giving is the first level, and receiving is the second. When you experience the flow of giving and receiving, you are at the third level. And when you contemplate your experiences in light of the highest goal so that you can bring this practice of giving and receiving more and more into your life, you have reached the fourth level.

Athena Katsaros worked with Julia Romaine to develop a program based on our creativity work for families of the victims of the 9/11 tragedy. As she worked with these widows, she experienced all four stages. "At first I was giving everything I had to give in the classroom," she said. "Afterwards I felt exhausted, physically and emotionally. I realized that I was giving without allowing myself to be refilled at the same time. I saw how the women were not needy, so I did not have to give everything without getting reenergized by them at the same time."

Athena decided to set an intention. "I decided to give absolutely everything I have to give and, at the same time, be filled up by their energy, enthusiasm and appreciation. This has been a big shift and has made the work so much more enjoyable and fulfilling."

But that wasn't all: When Athena told others about this shift she made into flow and appreciating the gifts she was receiving from these women, another flow occurred. She gave the gift of her experience, and others were inspired by it and gave back to her. For example, one woman, a widow herself, gave her own gift: "Your insight is so powerful," she told Athena. "I know how thick and powerful grief energy can be, and with the added energy from the notoriety of the event, it must be that much more so. To transform this energy to something generative is truly remarkable and inspiring."

Participate in the flow of giving and receiving and see what happens. You will be astounded.

The Struggle and Discovery of Being

Once you are committed to the quest for the highest goal, you also make a commitment to face life's struggles. And it seems, paradoxically, that the more you live this way, the more tests you experience. They are part of the journey that connects you with others and to generative leadership.

"Simply be." Whenever I hear or read that command— Simply be—I get a sense of relaxation, of just sitting. And indeed, meditation itself is a pathway to the highest goal; but the state of simply being has to be carried out in action.

You bring your state of being to the world when you take the risk to be your Self in what you do. And by doing that, you experience the highest goal and increase the probability that you will experience it in the future.

Once you quit striving so hard to be someone or something that you aren't, you can find your own brand of creativity and success, and transform what you already have within into something positive. You can be ordinary. Instead of fighting who and what you are, you simply get clear about it. The goal is to take the energy that exists and find harmony with it.

If someone criticizes you, for instance, listen to what they have to say. Consider, from your Self and from a state of Being, whether what they are saying has merit. Or is it simply coming from their VOJ or their condition at the present time?

If the latter is true, it is an opportunity to be compassionate and to honor what they are saying by listening and asking questions. Get into the flow of giving and receiving. Take an Aikido (the soft martial art that focuses on going with the flow of an attack) stance by acknowledging what they are saying. Perhaps you need to take some time away from this person, even if it is just a brief pause during which you can both just Be.

If there is merit in their criticism, however, you can try to alter your behavior, or you can reframe their criticism to see how the behavior they are criticizing is representative of positive qualities in you. If, for example, someone says you are manipulative, you can try not to be manipulative by acting in a way that is less intimidating and threatening. Or you can see your "manipulation" as being effective, astute and creative. You can acknowledge that you are attempting to serve people and meet their needs. While you are seen as manipulative, that is not your intention.

Remember that the inner source of any emotion or tendency is ultimately your Essence or Self. You can transform any input, even criticism from others or your own feelings of unworthiness, into an expression of your purest Self. This is not rationalization or self-deception. It is a way to hone your ability to Be in the world.

You can reframe any situation by accepting who you are, but don't fool yourself into thinking this is easy. You will struggle when you first attempt it because this takes discrimination. Then you will begin to see more possibilities than you can handle. If you stay with it, the process of being your Self becomes an adventure that leads to profound connection with others and with the highest goal.

The Secret in Action: Staying Alive

Jordan Gruber, a cofounder and editor of Enlightenment.com, tells a story about his own search for the highest goal. Contemplating the many paths to enlightenment he had undertaken or wanted to undertake, he asked a teacher for advice:

> "You want a plan," [the teacher] emphatically stated. "I'll give you a plan. Let go and let God! That's the only plan."
>
> He continued, "Look, you have a very strange notion of enlightenment. Some of the things that you've read about may happen to some of these people, but enlightenment, really, is just being who you are, how you are right now, without any shame, guilt, fear, or second thoughts. Just be who you are. That's enough. That's enlightenment"[1]

Living with the highest goal is a struggle, partly because it is unusual in a world that values external goals. In *The American Soul: Rediscovering the Wisdom of the Founders,* Jacob Needleman writes

> We do not understand the intrinsic contradiction of the spiritual search in the midst of the forces of life— sex, power and money. We trust the "official" religious saint, perhaps, who achieves sanctity through retreating from worldly life—the hermit in the desert, the monk in his monastery. And we understand, and therefore in a certain sense we trust, the man or woman engaged only in the outer life with

no spiritual motivation at all. But we do not grasp the co-existence of these two directions in any individual or in ourselves.[2]

The world needs more people who travel the spiritual path toward the highest goal as they face life's challenges. If we get stuck with what others tell us to do, if we believe that what we own and achieve and look like determines whether we are whole and valuable, then we are caught in an insignificant life with limited contribution and little juice—love, passion and compassion.

People may ask, "Why am I here in this life?" But among those who ask that question, relatively few recognize that the ultimate answer is to achieve the highest goal. Even fewer have the perspectives and heuristics to guide them on their way.

But you have them now. Please don't stop. Live by the secrets you have found here, and make these discoveries your own. Don't let fear stop you. Stay on your path and come alive.

Appendix:
Continue the Journey

A s you continue on your path to the highest goal, you will
hit obstacles that can be enriching but will also require you
to draw on your greatest resources. The following are suggestions for facing those obstacles and turning them into learning.

Reaffirm Your Highest Goal

As you continue on your path and learn more, take some time peri-
odically to consider the nature of your highest goal. Think of times
that you felt in connection with it, and celebrate those times. Write
a statement of your highest goal and commit yourself to it. Imagine
what it would be like to have more and more times in connection to
your highest goal. Then you have clarity as you face the challenges of
your life.

Swami Shantananda, a monk in the Siddha Yoga tradition,
puts this commitment in this way: "Since the moment I received
spiritual awakening, I have dedicated myself to the pursuit and the
attainment of the Self [living from a constant connection to the

divine within and without, his concept of the highest goal]. In my life, every other priority is secondary to that one great goal. So, before I read a book . . . I approach it with the light of my intention."[1]

If you can live with this sort of clarity and commitment, there is no question that you will receive the benefits of the highest goal.

Use Live-Withs

Tie any issues or opportunities you may have to topics within the chapters, and apply what you learn by practicing appropriate live-withs. If you have a time and stress problem, for instance, you would go to that chapter, specify your challenge, draw on the discoveries there, and then practice the live-with Don't Worry, Just Do It (or others found in Appendix B). Know also that you can come back to live-withs that you have practiced before and get more from them in whatever new circumstances you face and new insights you have.

Create an Expression of Your Self

When you get at a point of dryness or slow going, do an exercise that we do at the end our creativity course: Do a creative expression. Take some time, perhaps spread over a week or so, to consider how you might express your Self. This creative expression is to be a demonstration, or "picture," of your Self (and if you wish, how it integrates with your Work, relates to special challenges for you and live-withs and exercises that work for you). Its form is up to you. In the past, people have expressed themselves in the following ways: photography, sculpture, collage, mandalas; dancing, singing, playing music, storytelling; creating art, poetry, slides, movies or videos, crafts; performing skits and mime; preparing food and drink; participating in games or group activities; working puzzles; designing and producing furniture, clothes, web pages, wall- or ceiling-hangings.

You can decide whether you wish to actually show or perform this expression for anyone else. You will get more out of it if you do. And you'll be giving a gift to the people who see your creation. It will open them up to their own greatness and give them a new insight into you.

Many of the people who have done creative expressions for our programs still have copies of what they have done. They keep them in honored places in their homes or offices to remind themselves, in a small way perhaps, of whom they are and what they have to give to the world.

The variety and the heart with which people express themselves when they are given the task of bringing out their best always amaze me. Often they will do things they have loved to do in the past but don't do regularly anymore. Sometimes they will push themselves to do these activities, whether they have done them before or not, because they see this as an opportunity to take a leap, whether they are afraid or not, to be themselves.

One woman had been an accomplished pianist when she was younger but now played only occasionally. She composed a piece for the piano and recorded it. As it was playing, she recited a poem about her relationship with her mother just before she prematurely died, ending with the line, "A snowflake becomes brilliant in the sun just before it melts away forever."

One man was considering whether he would shift from his fast track in business to his love of coaching football and of working with young people and creating teams that work together. He was volunteering as a defensive line coach for a local college team at the time he took our course. He put together a film of highlights and tragedies of the season, combined with inspiring music. As he created this stirring presentation, he made a decision to coach, and his family supported him completely.

A Latin American woman created a beautiful collage and painting with a poem by Jorge Luis Borges exploring what he would do if he could live life over again. With tears in her eyes, the woman faced her art and addressed the poet (saying respectfully, "Señor Borges"), vowing she would live her life fully from her Self and not miss any chance to give her gifts to the world.

I consider it one of the blessings of my life that I have been present as hundreds of people have shared their creative expressions. When you develop a creative expression and share it, you are speaking from the heart. You are one with your Self and with others. You are giving a gift that you can carry with you on your journey. You are creating an experience of communion, with your Self, with God or whatever you call the grace that exists in the world.

More often than not, when you rise to the occasion of expressing your Self in a given period of time, you see the possibility of something greater in your life. You can live a life in which every moment has potential for connection, creativity and service. Eventually you see that this is one way to achieve the highest goal— to live every moment as a creative expression.

Make a New Kind of Business Card

Take some time to write your purpose and highest goal on a small card that you can put in your wallet as a reminder of who you are at core. Make this into a business card that represents the real you and your real job in the world, no matter what other people may think. Imagine that you might actually show this to someone who is important to you but doesn't really understand who you are or what you have to offer to the world.

Past participants of our courses have carried these Self/Work business cards for years. Jeff Skoll of eBay and the Skoll Family Foundation wrote "Remember what you want to do and that time is limited" on his card and had it in his wallet for over five years. When he got into trying times, this little card helped to get him on track by reminding him of his intention in each situation, even when that intention changed in focus from developing eBay's business to supporting social entrepreneurship programs that he felt were of value to the world. The card helped him to remember what he wanted to do and that his underlying intention was to express himself, especially through writing, in a way that would be of service to others—his highest goal.

You can create a card or reminder like this for yourself by putting your best qualities on one side of the card and then a type of business-card message with your name and the nature of your "business" on the other side. Make the business-card side fanciful and at the same time real to you. Then this card will be there to remind you of your commitment and to bolster you for the tough times. At some point you may forget about the card and live with the deeper reality that the card represents. Or you may want to revise it on the basis of your experience to reflect more relevant aspects of yourself that have come out as you have dealt successfully with the tests in your life.

One person, for instance, reached a point of clarity about his role of service in the world and the way he wanted to do it. He discovered that he loved the give and take of working with other people. In those situations he was willing to let go of himself and all pretension. On one side of the card he put "Laugh from the inside." And then on the business-card side he drew a picture of a medieval fool's cap with the inscription around it reading "Martin—a fool in the world." At the bottom he wrote in smaller letters "Available for weddings, parties, relationships, and serious work in the world."

This served him well as he went on his way. At one point, however, without dropping the sense of the first card, he made a new one to reflect his discoveries. He put on the back of this new card his most outstanding inner qualities—caring, compassionate, warm, honest, and wanting to bring out the best. Then on the front he drew a diver going into water with the message "Martin/The Diver: Going inside for the love and the truth."

Later he went even further in his sense of his contribution and the way he could offer it. On the back of the card he wrote "The speech of love is always silence." Then he created a business card on the front that pictured the Rock of Gibraltar in the center. Above this he wrote "Martin, the Rock," and he finished the card with "Immanent and Transcendent" on the bottom.

For him, this new card represented his increasing ability to be strong in his dealings in the world by coming from the power and the love of the silence within. He knew that to anyone else, the immanent and transcendent part might seem presumptuous, since in most traditions these are qualities we give to God or the divine presence. But he wanted to remind himself of his highest goal, connection to God, as he went about his day. In this way he felt he could serve others more purely. He kept this card in mind as he related to others and did his work, and it gave him a sense of something greater working through him. It gave him compassion in every moment.

So start this process for yourself. Forget about Martin, but remember the possibility that his story represents. Make one of these Live from Essence business cards. Carry it with you as you face life's tests and draw life's grace. Be open. Notice what happens and celebrate your tests. If you need to make a new card, make it. Always keep going for the highest goal.

Develop Your Lifetime Live-With

Perhaps you would like to continue to do one or another of the live-withs because it can help you to deal with your challenges as you continue on. Or you can make up your own live-with for your journey. Make it something short and provocative that will test you and make you work. Write a rationale for it and some ideas for how it might be practiced. Keep the whole thing to a page in length. The discipline of this length will spur your creativity and give your live-with energy. Then try living with your live-with for a while. Be conscious of what happens. Share this with others. And then you might want to try something new or go back to one of our live-withs. Keep playing with this as you face the tests life presents you.

One person saw how during her life she had almost always held back from really expressing herself and giving the gifts that she knew she had to give. She felt pain at the loss but became excited about the possibilities of facing life with this new sense of her Self and Work. So her lifetime live-with became "Live It Up." It infused her with energy and fun, which were parts of how she saw her Self.

I marveled at what she was able to do while living with this live-with, even though she had serious physical problems, ailing aged parents and limited financial resources. She developed a real estate practice while starting to teach in a charter high school. Then she entered a graduate program in transpersonal psychology. She concentrated on her ability in filmmaking in her thesis project, which was on bringing the spiritual into film. She started to substitute teach and always brought the message of this book and her Self and Work into her teaching at the secondary school level. Then she started a radio program for teens. That developed into a television program and the development of several film projects. Through all of this, she drew inspiration from Live It Up.

Another person saw how he frittered away time not tending to what was his real life work, which was to help others live with each other in community. He was inspired by the line from the Indian scripture, *The Bhagavad-Gita,* about the fruitlessness of doing others' work, even doing it well, while not doing one's own Work, or dharma, even if done poorly. He saw that often in his life, doing something well that wasn't really his work distracted him. So his lifetime live-with was "Do Your Duty." Somehow, he told me, putting that strong word, "duty," as part of his live-with made him see in each moment that he couldn't waste time. It reminded him that he had a duty in this lifetime that was his and his alone. His duty became a gift that he cherished. And he found, as he lived with this discipline, that it became easier to be himself in everything he did. Again, he was able to do so much that it was an inspiration to me.

One woman was touched by the death of her mother's best friend, who had been a sort of surrogate mother to her over the years. She dedicated a list of seventeen lifetime live-withs to her departed friend. They included Laugh a Lot, Focus on What Really Matters, and Live in the Present.

Once she created those possibilities, she was able to concentrate on them individually as situations arose. She went back to the list often at the end of the day to see what came up during that day. And now she is able to move more directly from the underlying aspects of who she is and the highest goal, especially when a test presents itself to her.

So do this for yourself, not as these other people have done it but in the way that is best for you. Develop a lifetime live-with that is right for you. Write a rationale and beginning instructions. And see what happens to your life as you live with it.

Have a VOJ Destroying Party

Many of us pack too much when we travel, and one thing you don't want to take with you on your journey to the highest goal is the VOJ, the Voice of Judgment. So write or draw the aspects of the VOJ or secret fears that you really don't want to take with you. Make them intense, because these are the remaining aspects of the VOJ that continue to trouble you.

Then destroy this paper in some way that is satisfactory to you—burn it, bury it, throw it into the ocean or a lake, take it to the dump, or do something with it to give you the sense that it won't be going with you on your journey. Make this a ritual. Acknowledge these aspects of your VOJ as not being you, as voices of others that will no longer affect you. But as you destroy them and give them back to the earth, have a sense that you are purifying not just yourself but also the universe—that you are creating an energy that will help you on your way.

Make a 10X Commitment

Living with your highest goal can give you a focus that will push you to be your Self and do your Work in ways beyond anything you've imagined. Take advantage of that potential by making a 10X commitment, a tenfold increase in your gifts to the world and in the corresponding fulfillment of your life and of those around you.

You'll find that when you make such a commitment your life doesn't change quantitatively; it changes qualitatively. Instead of doing more of what you've done in the past, you do fewer things that are more focused on what is right for you as a channel to the highest goal. When you think the highest of yourself and your potential, you begin to realize a life that wouldn't be possible otherwise.

When an owner of a video production business in the Midwest made a 10X commitment, he sold his business and went on a quest to use his skills and link to his highest goal in a way that would benefit mankind. After an extensive spiritual quest, he focused on this 10X commitment:

> *To receive, create and transmit Love's sacred stories in digital media, in partnership with the power and beauty of the Mother Earth, to the peoples of the Earth.*

[T]o catalyze waves of transformation in the world of business as we make the leap as a species to wholeness and balance in all things and an economy that looks out for the children seven generations from now.

He specified steps he would take, allies he would seek and checkpoints on his progress. Within two years, he was developing the kinds of digitally told and delivered stories that he envisioned in his commitment statement. He was creating them for all sorts of organizations—sometimes in corporate settings, often with organizations that were developing new models of sustainability and co-creative work. His stories, both in video and in live events, inspire and make a bridge between spiritual truths and everyday needs. He is affecting the practices of whole industries.

He and his wife are much in demand to facilitate and set the context for deep dialogues on business and new ways of relationship. This has enabled them to work together in programs that not only make them a decent living, but also put them at the forefront of making the kind of world transformation he envisioned for his work.

To create your own 10X commitment, first consider what you have learned from this book about who you are at core, your life's purpose and how you are moving toward the highest goal. Get a good idea of where you are now in terms of living from your essence and of connecting with your highest goal. Recall those times when you felt most alive, did things meaningful to you and experienced your essential qualities in life.

After spending some time in reflection and perhaps jotting some notes, answer these questions:

- What would my life be like if I made a tenfold
  increase in my contribution to the world around me?
- What would my life be like if the fulfillment I get
  from drawing on the highest goal was multiplied by
  ten?
- What commitments to change in my life would I
  have to make to achieve this tenfold increase?

Use whatever method of contemplation that works for you
to consider these questions. You can put these questions in your
mind, and then meditate and see what direction you get. Or you can
write these questions before you go to sleep, and see if you have any
illuminating dreams or if any answers come to you in the morning.
Or you can start by considering these questions, and then just writing for five to ten minutes and seeing what comes out. You have a
tenfold commitment within you at any time. You just have to be
open to it and state it.

Bill Veltrop, large systems change agent and innovator (in
the past with Exxon and with his International Center for Organizational Design and, more recently with his wife Marilyn, in their
Pathfinder Circles dialogue groups for generative leaders), is the fore-
most proponent of making a 10✕ commitment. He often suggests
using Native American practices and getting close to nature to move
toward the new way of thinking that is required to create this new
vision for your life.

When I participated with Bill and others in developing my
own 10✕ commitment, I focused on the core of my commitment
that I had developed over several years as we went outside to contem-

plate. I sat under a small red maple tree honing my commitment, meditating and contemplating to see if there was something new that would support my initial vision.

From that contemplation I developed the first part of my current commitment, which led to the writing and publishing of this book and other major changes in my life. It included bringing the highest goal into my life and others' lives through talking, training, observing, and writing. But the drive for doing those things came from a further connection to the highest goal that manifested as I sat there under the red maple tree.

I began to notice the leaves of the tree. They were a deep, almost purple red with many veins that shaped the leaves, brought them nourishment and made them miraculous to me. I held a leaf in my hand and closed my eyes. I sat there for some time and from inside I heard the "voice" of the tree giving me deeper insights than I thought I had. It said

You don't have to, Michael. You don't have to:

- *Be a beacon*
- *Do all these things*
- *Do anything*

Just be. Then do what is in front of you to do. Feel the comfort of it. I will provide.

Experience peace in you and then you'll find it outside also. The beauty of each of my leaves comes from the same beauty that is in you, too. My roots, flexibility and community are yours also.

You don't have to reach or strain, the leaves are within your grasp, provided for you, each perfect in its own way. Do what your being allows. You are part of my tapestry.

Allow the plan to manifest. Do what you can do; everything done with love is perfect. See the intricacy in my leaves. Do you think that you can do this on your own?

Take the leap. Especially at major transitions in your life, imagine what is possible with the highest goal. Ask yourself what it would mean to have a tenfold increase in your life. Commit to making that happen. And listen to the voice of your own maple tree. You'll always have abundant help for your journey. Accept it in whatever forms it takes.

Appendix:
Live-Withs

SOMETIMES WHEN I give people live-withs, I just give them the title without any instructions. They relate to the admonition with a sense of discovery based on what they know and need. They then create their own way of practicing the live-with. In many ways the results from this no-instruction approach are more profound because people are more resourceful and creative.

So below find a list of live-withs that you can use in this way, perhaps on the basis of the challenge it represents, or a need you have or maybe just because you like the sound of it. You'll see some that are already in this book, so you can get instructions for those. But in most cases, you're on your own.

To Develop Faith in Your Own Inner Resources
Have No Expectations
I Don't Know
If at First You Don't Succeed, Surrender
Let Go

To Diminish Your Inner Voice of Judgment (VOJ)
Psych Out the VOJ
Say Hello and Then Good-bye to Your VOJ
Destroy Judgment, Create Curiosity

To Move into Precise Observation
Be Awake
Everything Is New
Pay Attention

To Increase Your Use of Penetrating Questions
Ask Dumb Questions
What Questions of Wonder Will I Ask Today?
Quest!

Purpose/Prosperity Challenge
Do Only What You Love, Love Everything That You Do
Do Only What Is Easy, Effortless and Enjoyable
Be Ordinary
To Thine Own Self Be True
At This Moment, What Is Your Aim?
What Is Your Intention Now?

Time and Stress Challenge
Don't Worry, Just Do It
Don't Think about It
Be Bold
Walk into Fear

Relationship Challenge
See with Your Heart
Live with Compassion
See Goodness in Yourself and Others
Speak Up!
Collaborate

Listen
Forgive

Balance Challenge
Yes or No?
Ask Yourself If It's a Yes or a No
Everything in Life Is Either a Yes or a No
What Is Your Decision Now?
Recognize Your Decision Now

Challenge of Sharing Your Creativity
Become a Generative Leader
Participate in the Flow of Giving and Receiving
Be in the World but Not of It
Be Your Self, Do Your Work
Live in Essence
Amplify Positive Deviance
Trust

Miscellaneous
Be Honest with Yourself
Be Loyal to Your Own Values
Be Spontaneous
It's Up to You!
Keep It Simple
Poke, Prod, Test, Tweak
Seek Goodness in Yourself and Others
Stop and Listen!
Be Breathed, Be Loved and Listen
Be Prepared for Serendipity

Add Your Own:

Notes

Preface

1. Dominic Houlder in Kulananda and Dominic Houlder, *Mindfulness and Money: The Buddhist Path of Abundance* (New York: Broadway Books, 2002), p. xii.

Introduction

1. Keith H. Hammonds, "Q&A with Twyla Tharp," *Fast Company*, Number 75, October 2003, p. 42.
2. Don Wallace, "The Soul of a Sports Machine," *Fast Company*, Number 75, October 2003, p. 102.
3. Ibid.

Chapter 1

1. Quoted in *C. G. Jung Letters*, Vol. I: 1906–1950, ed. Gerhard Adler (London: Routledge & Kegan Paul Ltd., 1973).
2. Mahatma Gandhi, *An Autobiography: The Story of My Experiments with Truth* (Boston: Beacon Press, 1957), Part 2, Chapter XXVI.

Chapter 2

1. Recorded dialogue with Michael Toms, "From Monkey Mind to Clear Mind," New Dimensions World Broadcasting Network, Tape #2970, September 2003.
2. Lorna Catford, Ph.D., and Michael Ray, Ph.D., *The Path of the Everyday Hero* (New York: Tarcher-Putnam, 1991), p. 63.

Chapter 4

1. Pamela S. Mayer, "Wealth Experienced Requires Space," in Verna Allee and Dinesh Chandra (eds.), *What Is True Wealth & How Do We Create It?* (New Delhi, India: Indigo Press, 2004).
2. Paul Hwoschinsky, *True Wealth* (Berkeley: Ten Speed Press, 1990), pp. 23–32.

Chapter 5

1. Eleanor Roosevelt, *You Learn By Living* (New York: Harper, 1960), pp. 29–30.

Chapter 6

1. Scott Morrison, "The Silence of Hurricanes," *The Network,* August 1995, p. 3.
2. Jiddu Krishnamurti, *Talks and Dialogues* (New York: Avon Books, 1968).
3. Ram Dass, with Stephen Levine, *Grist for the Mill* (Santa Cruz: Unity Press, 1976), p. 27.
4. Leo Tolstoy, *Great Works of Leo Tolstoy,* trans. Louise and Aylmer Maude (New York: Harper & Row, 1967).
5. Ibid.
6. Ibid.
7. Harold Ferrar, "Greatness of Soul: Great Characters in Western Literature," *Darshan,* Number 71, February 1993, p. 21.

Chapter 7

1. Darria Sander-Wagganer and Thomas J. Kosnick, *Heidi Roizen Inc.* STVP1998-001, (Stanford, CA: Board of Trustees of the Leland Stanford Junior University, 1998), p. 11.
2. Ibid.
3. Curtis Sittenfeld, "The Most Creative Man in Silicon Valley," *Fast Company,* Number 35, June 2000, p. 276.
4. Sander-Wagganer and Kosnick, p.1.
5. Gale D. Webbe, *The Night and Nothing* (New York: Harper Collins, 1983).

Chapter 8

1. Jordan Gruber, "Average Enlightenment: Enlightenment as Possibility, Not Fantasy," *Enlightenment.Com Newsletter,* v.3.07.1, July 2003.
2. Jacob Needleman, *The American Soul: Rediscovering the Wisdom of the Founders* (New York: Jeremy P. Tarcher, 2003), p. 72.

Appendix A

1. Swami Shantananda, with Peggy Bendet, *The Splendor of Recognition* (South Fallsburg, NY: SYDA Foundation, 2003), p.16.

Selected Bibliography

Catford, Lorna, and Michael Ray. *The Path of the Everyday Hero.* New York: Tarcher-Putnam, 1991.

Chopra, Deepak. *The Spontaneous Fulfillment of Desire.* New York: Harmony Books, 2003.

Collins, Jim. *Good to Great: Why Some Companies Make the Leap . . . and Others Don't.* New York: Harper Business, 2001.

Collins, Jim, and Jerry Porras. *Built to Last.* New York: Harper Business, 1994.

Dass, Ram, with Stephen Levine. *Grist for the Mill.* Santa Cruz: Unity Press, 1976.

Gandhi, Mahatma. *An Autobiography: The Story of My Experiments with Truth.* Boston: Beacon Press, 1957.

Goleman, Daniel, Paul Kaufman, and Michael Ray. *The Creative Spirit.* New York: Dutton, 1991.

Houlder, Dominic. *Mindfulness and Money: The Buddhist Path of Abundance.* New York: Broadway Books, 2002.

Hwoschinsky, Paul. *True Wealth.* Berkeley: Ten Speed Press, 1990.

Isaacs, William. *Dialogue and the Art of Thinking Together.* New York: Doubleday Currency, 1999.

Krishnamurti, Jiddu. *Talks and Dialogues.* New York: Avon Books, 1968.

Maruska, Don. *How Great Decisions Get Made.* New York: AMACOM, 2004.

Mipham, Sakyong. *Turning the Mind into an Ally.* New York: Riverhead Books, 2003.

Needleman, Jacob. *The American Soul: Rediscovering the Wisdom of the Founders.* New York: Jeremy P. Tarcher, 2003.

Peck, M. Scott. *The Different Drum.* New York: Touchstone Books, reprint edition, 1998.

Ray, Michael, and Rochelle Myers. *Creativity in Business.* New York: Doubleday, 1986.

Ray, Michael, and Alan Rinzler, eds. *The New Paradigm in Business: Emerging Strategies for Leadership and Organizational Change.* New York: Tarcher/Perigee Books, 1993.

Ray, Michael, and John Renesch, eds. *The New Entrepreneurs.* San Francisco: Sterling & Stone-New Leaders Press, 1994.

Renesch, John. *Getting to the Better Future.* San Francisco: NewBusinessBooks, 2000.

Sawi, Beth. *Coming Up for Air.* New York: Hyperion, 2000.

Shantananda, Swami, with Peggy Bendet. *The Splendor of Recognition.* South Fallsburg, NY: SYDA Foundation, 2003.

Tye, Joe, with National Business Employment Weekly. *Personal Best.* New York: John Wiley & Sons, 1996.

———. *Never Fear, Never Quit.* New York: Dell, 1997.

———. *Your Dreams Are Too Small.* New York: Executive Books, 2002.

Webbe, Gale D. *The Night and Nothing.* New York: Harper Collins, 1983.

Index

nature and realization, 18,
162–164
Needleman, Jacob, 149–150
New Orleans (LA), 100–101, 107
Newman, Michelle, 115
The Night and Nothing (Webbe),
135–136
9/11 widows, xxii, 38–39, 146–147
notes. *See* writing

O

obstacles. *See* crisis; hindrances
oneness and connection
ignoring, 47–48
and others, 99–100, 111, 115
and sustenance, 163–164

P

Pathfinder Circles, 162
Participate in the Flow of Giving
and Receiving, 142–147
passion and success
and awakening of consciousness, 17–20
and comparison, 21–23
and right livelihood, 23–25,
67, 158–159
and sense of purpose, 25–29
and sub-optimizing, 20–21
traditional views of, 13, 16–17
patterns, 43, 45–47

Paul, Saint, 64
Pay Attention, 50
Peck, M. Scott, 108
perseverance, 1–4, 32–34
See also commitment
Personal Creativity in Business.
See Creativity in Business
personal illustrations
awakening of consciousness,
17–20, 28–29
commitment and long-term
growth, 59–60, 149,
157–158
crisis and perseverance, 1–3,
3–4, 32–34
dealing with fear, 47–48,
81–82, 88, 94–95
difficulty-to-insight cycle,
27–29
faith, 65–66
giving and receiving,
140–142, 143–145, 146–147
the hero's journey, 38–39
identifying highest goal,
11–12
importance of personal path,
xiii–xvi, 25–27, 44
lifetime live-with, 157–159
prosperity challenge, 63, 77
relating from the heart,
102–103
service, 72
shifts in perspective, 52,
56–57, 70, 71, 156–157

About the Author

MICHAEL L. RAY is the first John G. McCoy–Banc One Corporation Professor of Creativity and Innovation and of Marketing (Emeritus) at Stanford University's Graduate School of Business. A social psychologist with extensive experience in marketing communication and in developing generative work environments for companies and individuals, he has produced over one hundred publications, including ten books. Among them are two of the first books in the field of consumer information processing and two that helped establish and develop inquiry into new paradigm business.

His best-selling *Creativity in Business* (with Rochelle Myers) was named one of the nine "Greatest Business Books Ever Written" by *Inc.* magazine. *The Path of the Everyday Hero* (with Lorna Catford) garnered the title of the best business self-help book of the year, and *The Creative Spirit* (with Daniel Goleman and Paul Kaufman) was the companion book to the PBS series of the same name, which was inspired by his Stanford course, Personal Creativity in Business. He is at work on *Conversations on the Basics* in collaboration with teachers of his creativity course. He lectures and consults to organizations and groups worldwide and has served as a director of a major retailer, a food company, a catalog company, a start-up airline, a national cable systems company, an advertising agency, and four non-profit organizations.

Michael lives by his highest goal, which is to be in communion and in service with love. He finds the greatest tests and grace in pursuing that goal in his roles as a husband, as a father to six children, as a grandfather to eight grandchildren, and as a spiritual student and yogi who has practiced one path for over twenty-five years. He cohosts a twice-weekly chanting and meditation group in one of two homes designed and built by his wife, Sarah, in Santa Cruz, California.

Michael works with and supports a group of teachers he and his team have trained to offer the creativity course on which this book is based to individuals and organizations. These remarkable teachers provide a unique combination of in-person sessions, Internet delivery, conference calling, and coaching along with award-winning Creativity in Business software, which is continually being developed for uses in all sorts of settings. More information is available at http://www.michael-ray.com and at http://www.thehighestgoal.com. You can contact Michael at Stanford University and at mlray@stanford.edu.

About Berrett-Koehler Publishers

Berrett-Koehler is an independent publisher dedicated to an ambitious mission: Creating a World that Works for All.

We believe that to truly create a better world, action is needed at all levels--individual, organizational, and societal. At the individual level, our publications help people align their lives and work with their deepest values. At the organizational level, our publications promote progressive leadership and management practices, socially responsible approaches to business, and humane and effective organizations. At the societal level, our publications advance social and economic justice, shared prosperity, sustainable development, and new solutions to national and global issues.

We publish groundbreaking books focused on each of these levels. To further advance our commitment to positive change at the societal level, we have recently expanded our line of books in this area and are calling this expanded line "BK Currents."

A major theme of our publications is "Opening Up New Space." They challenge conventional thinking, introduce new points of view, and offer new alternatives for change. Their common quest is changing the underlying beliefs, mindsets, institutions, and structures that keep generating the same cycles of problems, no matter who our leaders are or what improvement programs we adopt.

We strive to practice what we preach--to operate our publishing company in line with the ideas in our books. At the core of our approach is stewardship, which we define as a deep sense of responsibility to administer the company for the benefit of all of our "stakeholder" groups: authors, customers, employees, investors, service providers, and the communities and environment around us. We seek to establish a partnering relationship with each stakeholder that is open, equitable, and collaborative.

We are gratified that thousands of readers, authors, and other friends of the company consider themselves to be part of the "BK Community." We hope that you, too, will join our community and connect with us through the ways described on our website at www.bkconnection.com.

Be Connected

Visit Our Website

Go to www.bkconnection.com to read exclusive previews and excerpts of new books, find detailed information on all Berrett-Koehler titles and authors, browse subject-area libraries of books, and get special discounts.

Subscribe to Our Free E-Newsletter

Be the first to hear about new publications, special discount offers, exclusive articles, news about bestsellers, and more! Get on the list for our free e-newsletter by going to www.bkconnection.com.

Participate in the Discussion

To see what others are saying about our books and post your own thoughts, check out our blogs at www.bkblogs.com.

Get Quantity Discounts

Berrett-Koehler books are available at quantity discounts for orders of ten or more copies. Please call us toll-free at (800) 929-2929 or email us at bkp.orders@aidcvt.com.

Host a Reading Group

For tips on how to form and carry on a book reading group in your workplace or community, see our website at www.bkconnection.com.

Join the BK Community

Thousands of readers of our books have become part of the "BK Community" by participating in events featuring our authors, reviewing draft manuscripts of forthcoming books, spreading the word about their favorite books, and supporting our publishing program in other ways. If you would like to join the BK Community, please contact us at bkcommunity@bkpub.com.